Volume 8

Final Respects
Into The Machine

Jim Russo
profjim@email.com

Collection of Plays – Volume 8   Jim Russo

Published by Deo Gratias, LLC – Detroit, MI

Copyright © 2023 by Jim Russo

All rights reserved. You may neither reproduce nor transmit any part of the contents of this book in any form or by any means, without the written permission of the publisher.

This book is a work of fiction. Names, characters, places, and incidents either are products of the author's imagination or are used fictitiously. Any resemblance to actual events or locals or persons, living or dead, is entirely coincidental.

Performing these plays is encouraged; although, you must obtain permission from the author in advance.

First Printing

Table of Contents

TABLE OF CONTENTS 3

FINAL RESPECTS 4

    CAST OF CHARACTERS 5
    ACT I SCENE 1 6
    ACT II SCENE 1 53

INTO THE MACHINE 101

    CAST OF CHARACTERS 102
    ACT I SCENE 1 103
    ACT I SCENE 2 140
    ACT II SCENE 1 161
    ACT II SCENE 2 176
    ACT II SCENE 3 201

Collection of Plays – Volume 8 Jim Russo

Final Respects

A Play in Two Acts

Copyright © 2023 E-mail: profjim@email.com

Cast of Characters

DAVE, (Groom-to-be) Man in his mid-twenties with nicely cut black hair. Dave is well-built and physically fit.

SAMANTHA, (Bride-to-be, goes by Sam), Woman in her mid-twenties with black shoulder length hair. Sam is an attractive, quick-witted woman.

ANNA (Sam's best friend, and maid of honor), Attractive woman in her mid-twenties with dark brown shoulder length hair.

CHRISTINA (Sam's bridesmaid), Attractive woman in her mid-twenties with dark brown shoulder length hair.

MR. WESLEY is a bumbling, elderly, well-dressed funeral director with thick horn-rimmed glasses. Strangely enough, Mr. Wesley is terrified of funeral homes.

ELIZABETH (Sam's Mom), An attractive woman in her mid-fifties with brown hair.

Extras and off-stage voices:
While a pronoun is assigned in the play, these roles can be performed by either males or females. These individuals appear once in the play and have few, if any, lines.

Scuba Diver
Mail carrier
Auto mechanic
Unseen women and man in the hallway
Carhop
Tennis player
Clown
Person pushing a shopping cart
Pastor

Act I Scene 1

(There is only one set in this play, the parlor of a funeral home.

Against the back wall, in the center of the stage is a double wide doorway which leads from this funeral parlor into a hallway in the funeral home. From the view of the doorway, the audience can see a conservatively wallpapered wall adorned with elegant lighting sconces.

Immediately inside the funeral parlor on the left side of the doorway there is a stand with a book for guests to sign and a stack of holy cards. Also, on the left side of the stage there are a total of six chairs assembled in two rows.

On the right side of the doorway, at a reasonable distance from the door, is a closed casket with a kneeler in front of it. A photo board, to the right of the casket, is close to the casket displaying photographs of the deceased. Also, there is the standard decor that one would expect to see in a funeral parlor, flowers, lamps, couches, small tables and so on.

The parlor is adorned on both sides with lavish floral arrangements which each have a note from the sender.

In this scene:

Dave, Mr. Wesley, Sam, Anna, Christina, Scuba diver, Mail carrier, Mechanic, three women heard off stage.)

DAVE
(Mr. Wesley is seen facing the audience standing by the entry way to a parlor drinking a big glass of chocolate milk. Mr. Wesley turns his head and pensively focuses on the casket to his right.

Visible through the open door, a man, who by all appearances looks like he is about to be married, dressed in a white tuxedo, can be seen walking back and forth in the hallway outside the funeral parlor. That man stops and approaches the funeral director who is now staring directly at the casket)
Can you tell me where….

MR. WESLEY
(Clearly startled. Mr. Wesley accidentally splashes the chocolate milk in his glass all over Dave's white tuxedo.)
Woo! This place gives me the heebie jeebies!

DAVE
(Looking at his stained white tuxedo. With frustration.)
Great!

MR. WESLEY
(Apologetically.)
Oh, I thought you were….

                              (Pauses.)
a ghost!

                              DAVE
                              (Trying to brush off his tuxedo.)

A ghost?

                              MR. WESLEY
                              (Pensively)

You know.
                              (Pointing to the casket when he says the word "residents".)
One of the residents.
                              (Puts emphasis on the word "are".)
After all, you *are* dressed in white.

                              DAVE
                              (Trying to brush off his tuxedo. Puts emphasis on the word "white".)
Yeah, it's my *white* tuxedo. I'm getting married today.
                              (Still trying to clean his tuxedo.)
Do you know which parlor Edna Murphy is in?

                              MR. WESLEY
                              (With delight points to the casket to the right.)
You found her, sir. She is in this parlor right here.
                              (Surprised. Looking at the chocolate milk stains on Dave's tuxedo.)
But why are you getting married in a dirty tuxedo?
                              (Dave glares and looks at Mr. Wesley and the chocolate milk that remains in the glass. With realization that he is responsible for the chocolate milk stains.)
Oh, I see. I really made a horrible mess, didn't I?
                              (Pauses.)

Don't you worry. I'll get your tuxedo looking as good as new in no time.

                      DAVE

Will it take long?
                      (Looks at his wristwatch.)
Because I'm getting married in about an hour.
                      (Pauses.)
I just wanted to stop in and quickly pay my respects to my future wife's Great-Aunt.

                      MR. WESLEY
                      (Reassuringly.)
Oh no, don't worry! We have an entire floor dedicated to cleaning garments.
                      (With confidence.)
I assure you; your tuxedo will be priority number one! It will be cleaned in no time at all!
                      (Motions with his hand as he starts to walk to the hallway.)
If you follow me, I'll get your tuxedo cleaned immediately!

                      (Dave follows Mr. Wesley out the door into the hallway heading off to the right and out of sight of the audience leaving the parlor vacant.

                      In a few moments, Sam enters the parlor from the left wearing a wedding dress and quietly walks up to the closed casket and bows her head reverentially for a few moments.

                      Sam, appears to be grieving, dabs her eyes with a tissue. She then looks around the parlor and notices the parlor is empty. She takes the opportunity to adjust a wedgie in her dress.

In a short while Dave quietly walks back into the parlor, wearing only boxer shorts, a T-shirt, a pair of socks and shoes. Dave approaches Sam sympathetically and gently placing his hand on her shoulder.)

SAM
(Sam is startled, jumps, and lets out a scream. Turns to see how Dave is dressed and lets out a second scream.)
What are you doing? Why are you dressed like that?

DAVE
Sam, you're not going to believe what happened!

SAM
I'll bet you're right!
(Agitated.)
What happened? Where is your tuxedo?

DAVE
(Takes a deep breath.)
Well, it all happened here about five minutes ago.

SAM
(Starting to get panicked.)
What happened five minutes ago?

DAVE
I came to see your Great-Aunt Edna, and….

SAM
(Pointing to the way Dave is dressed.)

Wearing your boxer shorts and T-shirt?
       (With agitation.)
A bit casual! Don't you think?

       DAVE
       (Smiles.)
Oh no, I….

       SAM
      (Covers her mouth in horror.)
You weren't naked, were you?

       DAVE
      (Somewhat defensively.)
Sam, of course not!

       SAM
      (Glaring at Dave.)
So? What happened then?

       DAVE
    (Pointing to the entrance of the parlor.)
I walked in,
      (Puts emphasis on the words "white tuxedo".)
wearing my *white tuxedo* and asked the funeral director if this was the right parlor for your Great-Aunt.

       SAM
The right parlor?

       DAVE
      (Nods affirmatively.)
Yeah.

       SAM
      (Still glaring at Dave.)

You didn't notice the neon sign outside the door?

        DAVE
        (Surprised.)

Neon sign?

        SAM
      (Pointing to the hallway.)

Yeah, the flashing neon sign right outside the door which has Edna's name displayed!

        DAVE
     (Shaking his head negatively.)

You're making this up!
       (With certainty.)
There is absolutely no way I'd miss a flashing neon sign!

        SAM
     (Continuing to point to the hallway.)

Go check it out, Sherlock!

        DAVE
     (Walks to the hallway and peers his head toward a sign not visible to the audience.)

I'll check it out, but there's no way, a....
       (Sheepishly.)

Oh, that flashing neon sign!

        SAM
      (Somewhat angrily.)

Besides!

        DAVE
     (Starting to walk toward Sam.)

Besides what?

        SAM

(Somewhat angrily.)
It's bad luck for you to see me in my wedding gown before the wedding!

DAVE
(Tilts his head and looks at Sam.)
As if seeing one another in a funeral home before the wedding isn't bad luck enough?

SAM
It's not my fault that Great-Aunt Edna died.

DAVE
(Trying to be comforting.)
I'm not blaming you....
(Pauses.)
It's just that this isn't the way I expected to prepare for the wedding.

SAM
(Walks toward the casket.)
Me either, Dave.
(Wistfully.)
Me either, Dave.

DAVE
(With compassion.)
I'm sorry for your loss, Sam.

SAM
(Nods in gratitude.)
Okay, so you didn't see the monstrously large flashing neon sign outside the door.
(Inquisitively.)
But what happened to your tuxedo?

DAVE
(With compassion.)

Well, since I didn't see the neon sign.

                        SAM
                  (Puts emphasis on the words "monstrously" and "flashing".)

The *monstrously* large *flashing* neon sign?

                        DAVE
                  (Somewhat annoyed.)

Yeah, that one.

                  (Points to the hallway where the light of the neon sign can be seen pulsating very brightly in the hallway for a few seconds.)

I didn't know if this was the right parlor, so I asked the funeral director if it was the parlor for Aunt Edna. When I asked him, he splashed me with chocolate milk.

                        SAM
                  (Incredulously.)

Splashed you with what?

                        DAVE

Chocolate milk.

                  (Pointing to where Mr. Wesley was standing.)

He was standing there drinking chocolate milk when I walked in.

                        SAM
                  (Uncertain.)

So?

                  (Pauses.)

Why would he splash you with chocolate milk?

                        DAVE

He said that I startled him. He told me that this place gives him the
                  (With emphasis.)

heebie jeebies.

SAM
(Shakes her head.)

The heebie what?

DAVE
(Trying to explain.)

The heebie jeebies.

SAM
(Looking intensely at Dave.)

Heebie jeebies?
(Still not understanding.)
What in the world are the heebie jeebies?

DAVE
(Still trying to explain.)

He was afraid.
(Motions around the room.)
You know.
(Shrugs.)
Because this place is a funeral home.
(Motioning with his hand to the casket.)
With dead people.

SAM
(Looking intensely at Dave.)
The funeral director is afraid to be in the funeral home?

DAVE
(Nodding.)
That's what he told me. Since I was dressed in my white tuxedo, he thought I was a ghost.

SAM
(Looking suspiciously at Dave.)

A ghost, huh?
(Somewhat frustrated.)
Okay heebie jeebie boy. Will your tuxedo be cleaned in time for our wedding?

DAVE
(Pointing to the hallway.)
Let me go check.
(Starts to walk toward the hallway.)
He told me it would be done soon!

SAM
I hope so, otherwise we'll have some very interesting wedding photos.

ANNA
(As Dave exists the parlor, he briefly crosses paths with Anna.)
Hey, Dave!

DAVE
Hey, Anna!
(Dave walks out of view to the right of the hallway.)

ANNA
(Takes a closer look at Dave before he exits. To Sam.)
Is Dave losing weight?
(Pauses.)
Something looks different about him.

SAM
It's a long story, Anna.
(Shakes her head.)
It's a long story.
(Walks over to give Anna a hug.)

Thank you so much for coming.

ANNA
(With sincerity.)
I'm so sorry to hear about your Great-Aunt.
(Looking over at the casket.)
Was she sick long?

SAM
No, she passed in her sleep….
(Pauses.)
After she and her friends returned from the bar.

ANNA
(Curiously.)
Did she have too much to drink?

SAM
(Wistfully.)
Oh no, but she knew how to live life to the fullest.
(Pauses.)
She made some interesting friends along the way.
(Pauses.)
Early in her life she was a hair stylist.
(Pointing to some pictures that are displayed on the photo board.)

ANNA
(Starts to walk to the photo board as Sam follows her and points to specific pictures.)
No way!

SAM
What?

ANNA

(Examining the picture and points to a picture as she names each individual.)

Your Great-Aunt was the hair stylist for Marilyn Monroe,

(Points to another picture.)

Albert Einstein,

(Points to another picture.)

Elvis Presley, and

(Points to another picture.)

Queen Elizabeth II?

SAM
(Proudly.)

She was!

ANNA
(Shakes her head in amazement.)

That's amazing!

SAM

That was Aunt Edna.

CHRISTINA
(Walks into the parlor and walks over to Sam to express her condolences.)

I'm so very sorry for your loss, Sam.

SAM
(Embraces Christina.)

Thank you, Christina.

(Pauses.)

Thank you so much for coming.

CHRISTINA
(Walks over to Anna after embracing Sam and embraces Anna.)

Good to see you, Anna.

ANNA
(Gives Christina a kiss on the cheek and embraces her.)
Good to see you too, Christina!
(After they embrace, she points to the photo board and asks Christina.)
Did you know that Sam's Great-Aunt Edna was a hair stylist?

CHRISTINA
(Shakes her head negatively and then proceeds to examine the pictures.)
No way!

ANNA
That's what I said!

SAM
(Smiles.)
Aunt Edna was a livewire.
(Pauses.)
She had so many stories to tell.

ANNA
I'm sure of that!

SAM
(Pointing to a specific picture.)
Aunt Edna would always complain that Einstein never used the hair conditioner she gave him.

CHRISTINA
(Looking more closely at the picture.)
That would explain his wild hair!

ANNA
(Still trying to process the information.)

So, your Great-Aunt Edna knew Marilyn Monroe, Albert Einstein, Elvis Presley, and Queen Elizabeth II?

SAM
(Nodding affirmatively.)
Oh yes, they would all request Edna as their hair stylist!
(Lifts her finger in the air.)
There were other famous people too, but those pictures aren't on the photo board.

CHRISTINA
(With admiration.)
Your Great-Aunt Edna lived quite a life!

SAM
(Nodding affirmatively.)
Oh, she was a character.
(Pauses.)
She also had a lot of funny stories to tell too.

CHRISTINA
Really? Like what?

SAM
(Smiling.)
She was fond of telling the story about when she first met Elvis Presley when he had long shaggy hair.

ANNA
What did she say?

SAM
Edna mentioned that she and Elvis really hit it off when they first met.

CHRISTINA
The did?

SAM

Oh yes, Edna told the family how she and Elvis would joke with one another when they saw each other.

(Smiling.)

On one occasion she told Elvis Presley that he looked like a hound dog.

(Still smiling.)

She started humming while she was cutting his hair and said, "You Aint Nothing But a Hound Dog".

(Pauses.)

Shortly after that, Elvis released his hit "You Aint Nothing But A Hound Dog".

CHRISTINA
(Incredulous.)

You're making that up!

SAM
(Shrugs.)

Well, I wasn't there, of course.

(Pauses.)

But that's what Edna would tell the family at gatherings.

CHRISTINA

Were there other stories?

SAM
(Nodding affirmatively.)

Oh yes!

(Pauses.)

One of my favorites was the story she told about correcting Einstein.

ANNA
(Gasps.)

What?

SAM

(Nodding affirmatively.)
Of course, I don't know the details, but it was something to do with his....
(Tapping her lip, pondering for a moment.)
Oh yeah, the cosmological constant.
(Elaborates with hand gestures.)
Einstein wanted to remove the cosmological constant from his General Theory of Relativity, and my Great-Aunt Edna insisted that he keep it in.

ANNA
The cosmological what?

SAM
(Shrugs.)
I'm only repeating what Edna told me, but if I'm not mistaken it has something to do with, hmmm....
(Asks herself a question.)
What was that again?
(Once again tapping her lip, pondering.)
Oh, yeah, the expansion of the Universe.

CHRISTINA
Your Aunt Edna asked Einstein to keep the value in the equation?

ANNA
Einstein?
(Pauses.)
Albert Einstein?
(Sam nods affirmatively.)

CHRISTINA
And Einstein wanted to remove the value from the equation?

SAM
(Nodding in agreement.)

Yeah.

CHRISTINA
In the end Einstein was correct....
(Hesitates.)
Right?

SAM
(Nodding negatively.)
No, Edna was actually right about the cosmological constant, and Einstein kept it in the General Theory of Relativity.

ANNA
That must have strained their relationship.

SAM
Apparently, they remained friends long after that.
(Pauses.)
Even after she stopped cutting his hair.
(Reflectively.)
Although, he never used conditioner in his hair.

CHRISTINA
What about Marilyn Monroe?

SAM
(Turns to face Christina.)
Huh?

CHRISTINA
Marilyn Monroe. Your Great-Aunt cut her hair too?

SAM
(Nods affirmatively.)
She did.
(With modest emphasis.)

My Great-Aunt Edna even convinced Marilyn Monroe to be a platinum blonde.

ANNA
(Somewhat incredulous.)
She did?

SAM
(Continuing to nod.)
Yeah, Marilyn wanted to be a brunette.
(Pauses.)
But Edna convinced Marilyn that blondes have more fun.

ANNA
Wow, Sam, your Great-Aunt Edna was an amazing person.
(Pauses.)
Did she also keep in touch with her other clients?

SAM
(Nodding in agreement.)
All of them.

ANNA
Even the Queen?

SAM
(Continuing to nod.)
Oh sure, the Queen and Edna remained great friends.
(Pauses.)
Every time Edna would go to England, the Queen would insist that Edna stay at Buckingham Palace.
(Pauses.)
The Queen even gave Edna a Corgi which she kept for years.

CHRISTINA
The Queen of England gave your Great-Aunt a dog?

SAM
(Nods in agreement.)
Yup! That dog lived a good life.

CHRISTINA
How often would your aunt stay with the Queen in England?

MAIL CARRIER
(Before Sam can respond, a mail carrier walks into the parlor carrying a mail pouch of letters. Sam, Anna, and Christina focus their attention on the mail carrier.

The mail carrier looks through the mail pouch before extracting several pieces of mail. The mail carrier walks to the casket, lifts an unseen slot not visible to the audience, and deposits several pieces of mail into the slot. Before departing, he tips his hat to the three women.)

Good day, ladies!

(The mail carrier exits to the right into the hallway.)

CHRISTINA
(Sam, Anna, and Christina muster an awkward smile and wave at the mail carrier. Shaking her head and addressing her friends.)

Did you guys see that?

ANNA
(Also shaking her head.)

Yeah, that's a first.

How did he….

Why would he….

                (Sam, Anna, and Christina carefully inspect the casket unable to find the mail slot.)

                (Pauses.)

                DAVE
                (Enters wearing a pair of black pants that are clearly too short in length, and too large at the waist. Greets Christina.)

Hey Christina.

                CHRISTINA
                (Somewhat startled by Dave's appearance.)

Hey Dave.

                (Pauses.)

Why are you dressed like that?

                SAM
                (Responds to Christina shaking her head in frustration.)

Oh, it's a long story.

                (To Dave.)

Please tell me you're not going to wear that to the wedding.

                1st WOMAN IN HALLWAY
                (Before Dave can respond an unseen woman in the hallway can be clearly heard. She speaks with a very slight British accent and elongates the word "trousers".

                Mr. Wesley is visible to the audience in the hallway facing the woman that the audience cannot see.)

My deceased husband's *trousers* are missing.
>(With concern.)

I'm afraid my husband is catching a horrible draft.

>MR. WESLEY
>(Can be seen in the hallway trying to calm the woman.)

Don't worry, Ma'am.
>(Pauses.)

I'll find a pair of trousers for your husband.

>1st WOMAN IN HALLWAY
>(Mutters.)

Well, I certainly hope so.
My husband was a dignified man. The thought of him lying in state with no trousers in full display of God and everyone!
>(Mr. Wesley walks down the hallway out of site from the audience.)

>DAVE
>(Nervously looks over his shoulder. Clears his throat. To Sam.)

Sam, this place is amazing!

>SAM

What, the funeral home?

>DAVE
>(Nods in agreement.)

Yes! This place has five floors!
>(Holds up five fingers.)

Five!
>(Pauses.)

No wonder they call it a Mega-Plex!

>ANNA

I knew this place was big, but…

(Pauses.)

five floors?

DAVE
(Nods in agreement.)

Yup!
(Pauses.)

I haven't checked it all out yet, but as I'm waiting for my tuxedo to be cleaned, I've been
(Trying to sound mysterious.)

scoping it out.

CHRISTINA

Wow! That's a lot of funeral parlors!

DAVE
(Rubs his hands together.)

Well, it's more than just funeral parlors, there are....

SAM
(Interrupts Dave.)

What about your tuxedo?
(Pauses.)

Is it clean yet?

DAVE
(Trying to be reassuring.)

Don't worry Sam, the funeral director is seeing to it himself.
(Without saying a word, Sam points to the hallway.)

Let me check again.
(Starts to walk to the hallway.)

It should be ready any minute now.
(Points to the hallway.)

I'll be right back.

SAM

(Pointing to her wristwatch.)
We don't have a lot of time, Dave. So, please don't get distracted...
(Puts emphasis on the word "again".)
again!

                          DAVE
(In the hallway. Blows Sam a kiss.)
I'm on it, Sam. I'll be back in a jiffy.
(Off stage.)

                       CHRISTINA
(Walks over to sign the guest book. Before she gets to the guest book a scuba diver complete with an oxygen tank and flippers on his feet walks up to the guest book. The scuba diver takes off his mask and hands it to Christina to hold. Christina obliges. The scuba diver signs the guest book. Reaches out his hand to retrieve his scuba mask.)
Thank you very much Miss.
(Nods in appreciation.)
Have a good day.

                       CHRISTINA
(Clearly caught off guard.)
You too.
(Shrugs and looks to Sam and Anna.)
What was that about?

                          SAM
(Shrugs.)
Beats me!
(Pointing to the casket.)
I know that Aunt Edna had some interesting friends.

                          ANNA

                    (Goes back to the photo board. Pointing at a picture.)

Is this….

                    (To Sam.)

Is this your Aunt Edna with Neil Armstrong?

                    SAM

                    (Shrugs.)

More than likely.

                    (Looking at the picture that Anna was pointing at.)

Yeah, that's Edna and Neil Armstrong.

                    CHRISTINA

                    (Finishes signing the guest book and walks to the photo board.)

Let me see.

                    (Examines the picture.)

How did your Great-Aunt Edna know Neil Armstrong?

                    (Pauses.)

I thought she was a hair stylist.

                    SAM

She was, but….

                    (Pauses.)

Edna was involved in a lot of things after working as a hair stylist.

                    ANNA

Like what?

                    SAM

Edna was involved in the Moon Mission.

                    CHRISTINA

The Moon Mission? Doing what?

                    (Pauses.)

Cutting the astronauts hair?

SAM
(Nodding her head negatively.)
Oh no, NASA had her training the astronauts for the Moon missions.

ANNA
But why?
(Pauses.)
What does a hair stylist have to do with preparing for the Moon?

SAM
Edna only started as a hair stylist.
(Pauses.)
She had a fascinating career at NASA after that.
(Pauses.)
Actually, NASA put her in charge of teaching the astronauts what to do on the surface of the moon.

CHRISTINA
Your Great-Aunt Edna?
(Pauses.)
But why?

SAM
As I recall, it has something to do with a book she wrote.

ANNA
A book she wrote while she was a hair stylist?

SAM
(Nods affirmatively.)
Yes!
(Lifts her finger in the air.)
For a while her book was on the New York Times best seller's list!

ANNA
Did you ever read the book?

                        SAM
                (Nods negatively.)
As a child I remember Edna reading me excerpts from her book, but I never actually read the book.
                (Pauses reflectively directing the question to both Anna and Christina.)
Did either of you ever watch a recording of the Moon landing?
                (Anna and Christina both nod affirmatively.)

                        CHRISTINA
Many times.

                        SAM
Do you recall what Armstrong said a couple of seconds after he stepped on the Moon and said "One small step for man. One giant leap for mankind"?

                        CHRISTINA
                (Nods negatively.)
Not really.

                        ANNA
                (Also nodding negatively.)
Me either.

                        SAM
                (Lifts a finger in the air.)
Well, when you listen to it again, you will hear Armstrong say.
                (Using air quotes.)
Edna, you were right! It's exactly the way you described it.

                        CHRISTINA
                (Anna and Christina exchange puzzled glances.)
No way!

                    (Cocks her head and gives Sam a suspicious look.)

Are you being serious?

                    SAM

Absolutely!

                    (Shrugs.)

The next time you watch the video, check it out!

                    (Pauses.)

You can't miss it. Armstrong says it very clearly, he even….

                  AUTO MECHANIC
                    (Before Sam can complete her sentence, an Auto Mechanic wearing a baseball cap walks into the parlor with a rag tucked into his pants. The mechanic is also carrying a small flashlight, pressure gauge, and battery powered screwdriver. The mechanic quietly walks to the casket, pulls out an unseen dipstick, examines the dipstick, before wiping it off and replacing it. He nods to the ladies.)

Hello, ladies.

                    (Sam, Anna, and Christina are somewhat bewildered and smile at the mechanic in response continuing to watch him.)

I won't be long, I promise.

                    (Uses a flashlight to inspect the underside of the casket. Uses the battery-operated screwdriver at various locations underneath the casket. The sound of a well-tuned engine is briefly heard coming from the casket.)

Ah, that's better.

>   (Starts to hum as he checks air pressure
>   at various points of the casket. Taps the
>   top of the casket. Sounding satisfied.)

Everything seems to be in tip-top shape.

>   (Removes and tips his hat to Sam, Anna,
>   and Christina. Cheerfully.)

Have a good day, ladies!

>   (Sam, Anna, and Christina still
>   bewildered, nod and wave good-bye to
>   the mechanic.)

> ### CHRISTINA
> (Shrugs.)

What in the world was that about?

> ### SAM
> (Looking at Christina and Anna.)

I must admit, that did seem a little odd.

> ### ANNA
> (Sam, Anna, and Christina walk over
> and inspect the casket.)

Where did he pull that dipstick from?

> ### CHRISTINA
> (Also inspecting the casket.)

Yeah, and what was he measuring?

> ### CHRISTINA

And the sound of the engine?

> (Also inspecting the casket.)

Where did that come from?

> ### SAM
> (Gives Christina and Anna a perplexed
> look.)

I have no idea.

(Pauses.)
Should we ask the funeral director?

                        ANNA
                 (Pointing to her wrist.)
We've got to get to the church for your wedding soon, Sam.
                 (Pauses.)
I don't think we'll have time.

                        SAM
                 (Nods in agreement.)
Yeah, as soon as Dave gets back with his tuxedo, we'll head over to the church.
                 (Looking pensively saying "man of the hour" with frustration.)
By the way, where is the *man of the hour*?
                 (Frustrated.)
I swear I'm going to wring his neck when I see him.

                        ANNA
                 (Walks over to the photo board and points to a picture.)
Oh Sam, this picture of your Great-Aunt is so cute!

                        SAM
                 (Sam and Christina walk to the photo board.)
Which one?

                        ANNA
                 (Continuing to point at the picture.)
The picture where Edna is teaching a young boy how to play the piano.

                        SAM
                 (Examines the photo.)
Oh yeah, that's Edna teaching Elton how to play the piano.

CHRISTINA

Elton?

(Hesitates.)

As in Elton John?

SAM
(Nods in agreement.)
Yeah, Elton John was such a cute little kid in that photo.

CHRISTINA
(Incredulous.)
You're telling us that your Great-Aunt Edna taught Elton John how to play the piano?

SAM
(Nodding in agreement.)
Yeah, she had a certain way about her.
(Shrugs.)
Of course, Elton was a gifted pupil.

ANNA

Was this after she worked at NASA?

SAM
(Nodding in agreement.)
Yeah, Edna was a person of many talents.
(Shrugs.)
She was never afraid to try new things.
(Continuing to nod in agreement.)
Edna had a lot of jobs and met a lot of people in her life.
(Pauses.)
She loved to teach children how to play sports.

CHRISTINA
(Pointing to a different picture.)
It looks like your Great-Aunt taught children how to play soccer too.

SAM
(Looking at the picture.)
She certainly did.
(Takes a closer look at the picture.)
Oh, that's Edna and Lionel Messi.

ANNA
(Shaking her head in disbelief.)
Messi?

CHRISTINA
(Chimes in.)
Lionel Messi the soccer legend?

SAM
(Nodding in agreement.)
Yup, Edna taught young Lionel how to play soccer. She had such a time having him focus on his footwork.
(Noticing that Anna and Christina are looking at each other in disbelief.)
That's not the only athlete that Edna taught.

ANNA
(In a state of disbelief.)
It's not?

SAM
(Scanning the photo board for a picture.)
Ah, here it is.
(Taps the photo.)
Do you guys know who this is?

CHRISTINA
(Anna and Christina shake their heads negatively.)
No.

SAM
(Continuing to tap the photo.)
It's Edna with Michael Phelps.

CHRISTINA
(Both Anna and Christina take a closer look at the photo.)
Michael Phelps, the Olympic gold medalist?

SAM
(Smiling.)
Yup!
(Starts to chuckle.)
Would you believe that before Michael met Edna he was afraid of the water?

ANNA
(Pointing to the photo.)
The future Olympic gold medalist swimmer was afraid of water?

SAM
(Nodding in agreement.)
Yeah, he hated to have his head under water.
(Pauses.)
But after Edna got his trust, I guess you can say the rest is history.

MR. WESLEY
(Walks in carrying an enormous floral display which he sets down in an empty location.

Before exiting the parlor, Mr. Wesley bows to Sam, Anna, and Christina and addresses them.)
Ladies.
(Mr. Wesley exits the parlor.)

ANNA
(Looking at the floral arrangement with amazement.)

Wow!

(Pauses.)

I've never seen a larger floral arrangement in my life!

(Shaking her head in disbelief.)

That floral arrangement is worth more than my car!

CHRISTINA
(Sam, Anna, and Christina start walking toward the floral arrangement.)

Let's see who it's from.

SAM
(Reads the note that came with the flowers.)

Oh, that's so sweet.

ANNA
(With anticipation.)

Who is it from?

SAM
(Hands the note to Anna. Surprised.)

Elon Musk.

CHRISTINA
(Incredulous.)

No way!

ANNA
(Hands the note to Christina who reads the note aloud.)

Dear Edna, I owe everything to you and your brilliance. With much love and gratitude. Elon Musk.

SAM
(With melancholy.)
She treated him like a son,
(Pauses.)
and he adored her.
(Pondering.)
Would you believe that Telsa was not Elon's first choice for his auto division?

CHRISTINA
(Nodding her head negatively.)
It wasn't?

SAM
(Nods her head negatively.)
No, he wanted to name the car after Edna.
(Shrugs.)
But Edna convinced him to name the car company after Tesla.

CHRISTINA
(Walks over to another large bouquet and reads the attached note.)
To a dear friend and national treasure, The President, and First Lady.

ANNA
(Walks over to the next large bouquet and reads the attached note.)
A life well lived, His Holiness The Pope.

CHRISTINA
(Walks over to another large bouquet and reads the attached note.)
You've always been my inspiration, Jeff Bezos.

ANNA
(Looks over at Christina.)
How come we never heard of Sam's Great-Aunt before?

                          CHRISTINA
                 (Shrugs and shakes her head negatively.)
Beats me.
                 (Looking at the massive floral
                 arrangements.)
It seems like we're the only two who never heard of Edna.

                            SAM
Well, she did like to keep a low profile.

                           ANNA
Mission accomplished.

                           DAVE
                 (Enters the parlor wearing a fancy
                 ruffled white shirt also sporting a
                 flamboyant pair of glasses. With
                 excitement, addresses the group.)
This place is so awesome!

                         CHRISTINA
                 (To Dave.)
Dave, Did you ever meet Sam's Great-Aunt Edna?

                           DAVE
                 (Shakes his head negatively.)
I was supposed to meet her once, but...
                 (Thinks for a moment.)
She was on an expedition to climb Mount Everest, or something.

                           ANNA
                 (Incredulous.)
How long ago was that?

                           DAVE
                 (To Sam.)

That was last May, right Sam?

                    SAM

No, last May was when she was conducting the peace talks in the Middle East.
                         (Pauses.)
I think she climbed Everest last September.
                                   (Looking at what Dave is wearing.
                                   Anna and Christina exchange glances
                                   and shake their heads in disbelief.)
By the way, I notice you're not wearing your tuxedo yet.

                    DAVE

I just checked, and they told me they were almost done.
                              (With delight pointing to his feet.)
They're going to polish my shoes too!

                    SAM
          (Shakes her head and points at Dave.)
I hope your tuxedo is cleaned soon, because you don't want to get married wearing that, do you?

                    DAVE
          (Shaking his head negatively. Softly.)
No.

                    SAM
          (Shaking her head with frustration.)
I certainly hope not!

                    DAVE
          (Trying to offer an explanation.)
These clothes are just temporary until the tuxedo is ready.

                    SAM
          (Pointing to her wristwatch.)

Do you have any idea how much longer it will take before your tuxedo is ready?

          (Shrugs and lifts her right hand.)

Five minutes?

          (Shrugs again and lifts her left hand.)

Ten minutes?

          DAVE

They told me that it is almost ready.

          2nd WOMAN IN HALLWAY
          (While Mr. Wesley can be seen in the hallway engaged in conversation with an unseen woman in the hallway the rest of the cast speak among themselves, either focusing on the photo board or investigating the casket.

          The woman seems to be very agitated.)

I recall that my husband had a shirt on earlier today!

          MR. WESLEY
          (Dave walks away from view of the hallway and nervously looks toward the hallway.)

I assure you, Madam, we will locate your husband's shirt.

          2nd WOMAN IN HALLWAY
          (Still agitated.)

The white ruffled shirt he was wearing was his favorite shirt!

          (Pauses.)

My Herbert is now laying there with his bare chest exposed to all the world!

          MR. WESLEY

(Nods with understanding to the unseen woman. Attempts to reassure the woman.)

I'll see to it that his shirt is located immediately.

3rd WOMAN IN HALLWAY
(As Mr. Wesley concludes the conversation with the woman he was speaking with, he takes a step into the parlor. Dave attempts to conceal himself. Mr. Wesley does not go far before another unseen woman engages him in conversation.)

Do you know what happened to my husband's glasses!

MR. WESLEY
(Returns to the hallway to address the woman who was questioning him.)

Excuse me, Ma'am?

3rd WOMAN IN HALLWAY

My husband Thaddeus had glasses!
(Pauses.)
He was wearing them earlier. Where did they go?

MR. WESLEY
(Reassuringly.)

Oh, I see.

3rd WOMAN IN HALLWAY
(Agitated.)

Well, my Thaddeus can't see a thing without his glasses.
(With emphasis.)
They are prescription glasses, and Thaddeus needs them.
(Pauses.)
Besides, the family won't recognize Thaddeus in the casket without his eyeglasses.

(With frustration.)

He wore them everywhere.

MR. WESLEY
(Continues to be reassuring.)

Don't worry, Ma'am, I assure you I will locate the glasses and return them to your husband.

3rd WOMAN IN HALLWAY
(In a huff.)

Well, see that you do!

MR. WESLEY
(Respectfully.)

Of course, Ma'am!

SAM
(As the conversation ends in the hallway, the conversation in the parlor continues. To Dave.)

Every time you come back you keep telling me that the tuxedo is almost ready.

DAVE
(Trying to explain.)

Sam, that's what they are telling me.
(Shrugs.)

Each time I go to check on them they are busy working on the tuxedo.
(Trying to sound optimistic.)

It can't be too much longer.

SAM
(Pointing to his glasses.)

When did you start wearing glasses?

DAVE
(Takes the glasses off and examines them.)

Yeah, they're cool, huh?

SAM

Cool?

(Pointing to his glasses.)

Those glasses?

(Asks Anna.)

Anna, do you think Dave's glasses are cool?

ANNA

(Trying to be polite. Pointing to the glasses.)

Umm, you mean those glasses?

(Asks Christina.)

Christina, do you think Dave's glasses are cool?

CHRISTINA

(Sincerely.)

Sure.

(Starts to chuckle.)

If his name was Liberace!

DAVE

(Sounding hurt.)

Really?

CHRISTINA

(Looking around the parlor.)

Well, I don't know.

(Starting to chuckle again.)

Why don't we go find a piano where you can sit and model your glasses?

ANNA

(Also starting to chuckle.)

That sounds like a good idea.

(Looking at Dave.)

What do you think, Liberace?
                    (Clears her throat.)
I mean Dave.
                    (Anna and Christina start to laugh.)

                    DAVE
                (Sounding hurt.)
Man, you guys are a rough crowd.

                    SAM
                (Bluntly.)
Dave, those glasses look ridiculous!
                (With agitation.)
While I hate to be a party pooper, let me remind you that we don't have a lot of time before the wedding is supposed to start.

                    DAVE
                (Trying to calm Sam.)
I'm just killing time while my tuxedo is getting cleaned.

                    SAM
                (Mutters under her breath.)
Time may not be the only thing getting killed.
                (Speaking normally, clearly frustrated. Cocks her head and looks at Dave.)
How much longer will your tuxedo take?

                    DAVE
                (Pats Sam on the hand.)
I just checked. I was told it was going to be any minute now.

                    SAM
                (Still agitated.)
I hope so!

                    ANNA
                (To Dave.)

You've been checking this place out while they clean your tuxedo?

DAVE
(Nods affirmatively.)
I have, and this place is so awesome!
(To the group.)
You all need to check it out!

CHRISTINA
(To Dave.)
What could be so special about a funeral home?

DAVE
There is so much, you really need to see it for yourself.

CHRISTINA
(Struggling to understand.)
This funeral home?

DAVE
(Nods affirmatively.)
Absolutely!
(Cautions.)
You may have to wait a while,
(Pointing up.)
because right now a fourth-grade class is having a field trip on the third floor.

CHRISTINA
(Struggling to understand.)
What? Here?

ANNA
(Also struggling to understand.)
Why would a fourth-grade class take a field trip to a funeral home?

DAVE

(With excitement.)
Oh, the kids love it!
(Pauses.)
This place has so much to offer.

ANNA
What could a funeral home offer a fourth-grade class?

DAVE
Oh, man!
(With excitement.)
All the hot dogs, cotton candy….

ANNA
Wait! Wait!
(Pointing to the ground.)
This funeral home?

DAVE
(Nods in agreement.)
Yes, and free scoops of gelato.
(Shakes his head negatively.)
Not ice cream.
(Says "gelato" with almost sacred emphasis.)
Gelato!

SAM
(Laughs.)
I think your brain has turned to gelato!
(Shaking her head.)
Are you sure you didn't hit your head when the funeral director spilled the chocolate milk on you?

DAVE
(Nods negatively.)
No, Sam, honestly.

(Pauses.)
This place is so cool! We should come back here after the wedding.

SAM
(Clearly frustrated. Says "gelato" angrily.)
I swear if you spill *gelato* on your tuxedo once you get it back,
(Points to Dave.)
you'll be the next customer here!

DAVE
(Trying to calm Sam.)
Sam, what kind of fool do you take me for?

SAM
(Cocks her head and looks at Dave.)
Is this multiple choice?

DAVE
(Trying to calm Sam.)
Sam, I'm sure the next time I go down to check on my tuxedo, it will be ready.

SAM
Okay, please go and check on it then.
(Pauses.)
Unless you put on the tuxedo in the next couple of minutes, there won't be a wedding.

DAVE
(Shrugs.)
Sam, I was just trying to occupy myself while I was waiting.

ANNA
(Trying to diffuse the tension.)
So, are we leaving for the church after Dave gets his tuxedo?

SAM
(Nods affirmatively.)
Yup, that's all we're waiting for.

CHRISTINA
You've got everything you need for the wedding, right Sam?

SAM
I do.
(Clears her throat and uses her thumb to point at Dave.)
All except for a properly dressed groom, that is!

ANNA
(Still trying to calm Sam.)
Okay, let's go over the list.
(Pointing to Sam's wedding gown.)
Of course, you have your wedding gown.

SAM
(Nods affirmatively.)
Yup.
(Glares at Dave.)
One without chocolate milk stains!

CHRISTINA
The flowers are at the church.

SAM
Yup.

CHRISTINA
Anna and I have our bridesmaid dresses on.

SAM
Yup.

ANNA
(Lifting a finger and says "Yup" with each item Anna mentions as Sam displays the item which meets the criteria except for the last item.)

You've got something old

(Pauses.)

something new

(Pauses.)

something borrowed

(Pauses.)

something blue.

SAM
(Somewhat panicked.)

Oh no!

ANNA
(Perplexed.)

What?

SAM
(In a full panic.)

I don't have something blue!

DAVE
(Trying to sound chivalrous.)
Don't worry, my lady, I shall return with something blue!

(Blackout. End of Act 1 Scene 1.)

Act II Scene 1

(Same set as Act 1.

In this scene:
Dave, Mr. Wesley, Sam, Anna, Christina, Elizabeth, Man and Women off stage, Tennis Player, Carhop, Person pushing a shopping cart, Clown, Pastor.)

DAVE
(Sam, Anna, and Christina are gathered in the funeral parlor. Dave dramatically enters the funeral parlor.

Dave is now wearing a Bolo Hat and a tie around his neck. Dave walks up to Sam triumphantly extends his hand to Sam and bows at the waist and exclaims.)

Something blue, my lady!

SAM
(Enthusiastically examining the bracelet.)

Dave, this is beautiful!
(Incredulous.)
How did you? Where did you?

ANNA
(Looking at the bracelet.)

Christina, check this out!

CHRISTINA
(Sam, Anna, and Christina admire the bracelet. Gasps.)

Are those real diamonds?

> ANNA
> (Shaking her head in disbelief.)

They must be.

> (Pointing to various stones on the bracelet.)

The Sapphires are so brilliant!

> SAM
> (Getting somewhat emotional looking at the bracelet.)

Dave, this must have cost you a fortune!

> (Continuing to admire the bracelet.)

How long were you going to keep this a secret?

> DAVE
> (Soaking in the praise.)

I wanted to get you something special on our wedding day.

> SAM
> (Unable to take her eyes off the bracelet, Sam, Anna, and Christina continue to admire the bracelet. Sam shakes her head with admiring disbelief.)

Well, you succeeded, Mister!

> (Finally takes her eyes off the bracelet and looks at Dave.)

This is the most beautiful....

> (Focusing on the Bolo Hat on Dave's head. Startled, points to the hat on Dave's head.)

What is that ridiculous thing on your head?

> DAVE
> (Still soaking in the praise. Pointing to his hat.)

Oh this?

Pretty sophisticated, huh?

        (Expecting a positive response.)

ANNA
(Anna and Christina's attention is drawn to the hat Dave is wearing. Trying to keep from laughing.)

Yeah, real sophisticated.

CHRISTINA
(Also trying to keep from laughing.)

Oh, yeah.

(Trying to sound sexy puts emphasis on the word "sexy".)

Real *sexy* too!

SAM
(Shaking her head. Exchanging glances between the bracelet and the hat.)

If it's the Laurel and Hardy look you're going for, you nailed it!

DAVE
(A little hurt.)

Oh, come on.

(Genuinely questions.)

You don't like it?

ANNA
(Still trying not to laugh while sounding sincere.)

I like it, Stan.

(Clears her throat.)

Err…umm…I mean Dave.

CHRISTINA

(Also trying not to laugh while sounding sincere. Looks at Anna.)

You did mean Ollie, didn't you?

                    1st MAN IN HALLWAY
(Mr. Wesley can be seen on the left side of the hallway engaged in conversation with an unseen man while the rest of the cast speak among themselves, either focusing on the bracelet or looking at Dave's Bolo hat which he has removed.

The man seems to be very agitated.)

That bracelet is irreplaceable.

(With growing agitation.)

How could it have just vanished from my wife's wrist?

                    MR. WESLEY
(Reassuringly.)

I assure you, sir. We'll find the bracelet.

                    1st MAN IN HALLWAY
(With clear frustration.)

What kind of place are you running here?

                    MR. WESLEY
(Continuing to reassure the frustrated man.)

I'm sure the bracelet will be returned within the hour, sir.

                    1st MAN IN HALLWAY
(Ends the conversation in a huff.)

See that it is!

                    MR. WESLEY
(Can be seen in the hallway bowing to the unseen man.)

Please don't worry, sir. We'll find the bracelet and see that it is returned.

       4th WOMAN IN HALLWAY
      (The first man in the hallway can be heard muttering as he walks away.

      Mr. Wesley takes a few steps into the funeral parlor until he is drawn back to the left side of the hallway by a woman who is trying to get Mr. Wesley's attention. Dave skittishly does what he can to avoid contact with Mr. Wesley. Mr. Wesley turns to speak with the woman in the hallway.)

Sir? Sir?

       MR. WESLEY
      (Attentively addresses the woman.)

Yes, Ma'am?

       4th WOMAN IN HALLWAY
      (Timidly.)
Do you know what happened to my husband's Bolo Hat?

       MR. WESLEY

Bolo Hat?

       4th WOMAN IN HALLWAY
      (A little more confidently.)
Yes, my husband was wearing a Bolo Hat, and when I returned, the hat was gone.

       MR. WESLEY
      (Trying to sound reassuring.)
I'm sure we will be able to locate your husband's hat, Ma'am.
      (Confidently.)

I'll investigate it right now!

       4th WOMAN IN HALLWAY
      (Softly.)
Thank you, sir.

        MR. WESLEY
      (Bowing to the unseen woman.)
I apologize for the inconvenience, Ma'am.
      (Can be seen extending his hand to the unseen woman.)
I will locate the hat momentarily, Ma'am.

       5th WOMAN IN HALLWAY
      (Mr. Wesley takes a few steps into the funeral parlor until he is drawn back to the right side of the hallway by a woman who is trying to get Mr. Wesley's attention. Dave skittishly does what he can to avoid contact with Mr. Wesley. Mr. Wesley turns to speak with the woman in the hallway.)
Excuse me sir!

        MR. WESLEY
      (Attentively addresses the woman.)
Yes, Ma'am?

       5th WOMAN IN HALLWAY
Do you know what happened to my husband's tie?

        MR. WESLEY
      (With concern.)
Your husband's tie, Ma'am?

       5th WOMAN IN HALLWAY
      (Emphatically.)

Yes, my husband's tie!
    (With concern.)
It disappeared right after that woman walking the dogs strolled into my husband's parlor on the fourth floor!

    MR. WESLEY
    (Trying to console the woman.)
What did your husband's tie look like, Ma'am?

    5th WOMAN IN HALLWAY
His tie has his clan's tartan.
    (Puts emphasis on the word "was".)
After all, he *was* Scottish!
    (Dave hears the conversation, looks down to his tie with a tartan pattern. Tries to conceal the tie.)

    MR. WESLEY
    (Trying to console the woman.)
Your husband's tie should be easy to locate, Ma'am.

    5th WOMAN IN HALLWAY
    (With concern.)
Please find and return it to my husband before the bagpipers arrive.

    MR. WESLEY
    (Bows to the unseen woman.)
Please don't worry, Ma'am.
    (Extends his hand to the unseen woman.)
The tie will be returned before the bagpipers arrive.
    (Tries to sound reassuring.)
You have my word!
    (Walks out of view down the hallway.)

    CHRISTINA
    (Pointing to Dave's tie. Speaking to Dave.)

Oh, Dave, please excuse me.
> (Pointing to Dave's hat.)

I see you're not Laurel and Hardy.

> DAVE
> (With an air of restored dignity.)

Thank you, Christina.

> (Confidently.)

Finally, an ally!

> ANNA
> (Puzzled.)

He's not Laurel and Hardy?

> CHRISTINA
> (Starts to chuckle pointing to his tie. Feigning a modest Scottish brogue.)

No, he's a Scotsman.

> (Pauses. Still feigning a modest Scottish brogue.)

Aren't you lad?

> SAM
> (Clearly agitated.)

He's going to be a dead Scotsman soon if I don't see him in his tuxedo in the next five minutes!

> DAVE
> (Starting to walk toward the hallway. Pauses at the hallway looking in both directions to ensure Mr. Wesley is not present before proceeding.
>
> To Sam.)

The next time you see me, Madame, I'll be all dressed in white!

> SAM

(Clearly agitated.)
Stay away from the gelato!

ANNA
(Not loud enough for Dave to hear.)
'Ya might want to lose the hat, too!

CHRISTINA
(Not loud enough for Dave to hear.)
Not to mention the glasses!

SAM
(To Anna and Christina.)
I don't know what's gotten into him today!

ANNA
(Trying to calm Sam.)
He's got pre-wedding jitters.

CHRISTINA
(Chuckling.)
Years from now you'll look back on all of this and laugh.

SAM
Do you think so?

ANNA
You'll have some great stories to tell the kids and grandkids, that's for sure.

CHRISTINA
Grandkids?

ANNA
Sure!
(Chuckling.)
Of course, you and "Scottie" will have plenty of kids first.

SAM

I'm afraid that "Scottie"….
(Chuckling.)
I mean, Dave, will want to come here with the kids.

CHRISTINA

Yeah, Dave really seems to like this place.

ANNA

Do you think Dave was exaggerating about this funeral parlor!

CHRISTINA

How exciting can a funeral parlor be.
(Shrugs.)
Although maybe we should go check it out.

ANNA

Yeah, we might bump into some hot guys.

CHRISTINA
(Anna and Christina start walking toward the hallway. With enthusiasm.)

Count me in!

SAM
(Motions for Anna and Christina to return.)
We can always come back later, guys. Let's check it out then.
(Looks at her watch.)
We really need to get going soon!

ANNA
(Looks at her watch with a panicked look. Tries to sound reassuring.)

Don't worry, Sam,
(Looks toward the hallway.)

Dave will be right back and then we will be on our way.

CHRISTINA
(Also tries to sound reassuring.)
While we're waiting, tell us more about your Great-Aunt Edna.

SAM
(Walks to the photo board looks at various photos. Pointing to a specific photo.)
Oh, I don't know if you guys saw this one before.

TENNIS PLAYER
(Before Anna and Christina can look at the photo that Sam is pointing at, a woman dressed looking like she is ready to play tennis comes bouncing a tennis ball on her racquet as she walks up to the guest book

Christina glances over at the woman who is close enough to hand Christina the tennis racquet and ball. Politely asks.)
Would you mind holding these?

(Christina is so startled she can't offer a verbal response and reaches her hands out to accept the tennis racquet and tennis ball as the tennis player signs the guest book. Once she is done signing the book, the tennis player reaches her hands out to take the racquet and tennis balls from Christina. Cheerfully.)
Thank you!

(With a smile.)
Thank you very much!

CHRISTINA
(Still stunned musters.)

No problem.

TENNIS PLAYER
(Bounces the tennis ball on the racquet as she approaches the casket. Bows her head as she stands silently in front of the casket.

When she is done with her silent prayer, she gently taps on the casket with her tennis racquet. (the "Shave and a Haircut. Two bits" knock.) 'Bum-ba-da-bum-bum'.

From inside the casket a distinct 'bum-bum' tapping can be heard. The tennis player turns to the ladies and says.)

She was such an amazing person.
(Sympathetically.)

I'm so sorry for your loss.

(Without exchanging a word, Sam, Anna, and Christina nod to acknowledge the woman.)

ANNA
(Sam, Anna, and Christina are speechless for a moment. Anna finally breaks the silence.)

Did you guys...
(Hesitates.)

Did you guys hear that tapping from inside the casket?
(Sam and Christina are still in stunned silence.)

Guys?

CHRISTINA
(Shaking her head.)
There is no way the knocking came from inside the casket!

SAM
(Struggling for an explanation.)
It must have been....
(Cautiously approaches the casket with Anna and Christina.)
It must have been....

ANNA
(Softly.)
You don't think....

DAVE
(Returns to the parlor wearing his tuxedo minus the jacket.)
Well, the only thing left is the jacket, and then we're out of here!
(Does not get a response from the women who continue to stare at the casket. Says the next line a little louder.)
Sam, all I need is the jacket, and then we can head off to the church.
(Still no response.)
Sam?

SAM
(As if coming out of a trance.)
Dave, go and stand by the casket.

DAVE
(Uncertain of Sam's intent.)
This is an odd time and place for a photo, isn't it?

ANNA
(Still standing close to Sam and Christina points to the casket.)

No, we're not going to take a photo.
>(Continuing to point at the casket.)
Just go and stand by the casket.

                DAVE
>(Shaking his head while he makes his way to the casket.)

I feel like I'm being set up.

>(Dave is now next to the casket.)

              CHRISTINA
>(Softly.)

Okay,

>(Makes a fist with her hand and motions knocking.)

and knock on the casket.

                DAVE
>(Baffled.)

Do what?

                SAM
>(Motions to the casket.)

Knock on the casket.

                DAVE
>(Still uncertain.)

Why?

                SAM
>(Makes a fist with her hand and motions knocking.)

Knock on the casket.

              DAVE
>(Mutters.)

Rather disrespectful, don't you think?

SAM
(Cocks her head with mild agitation.)

Just do it, Dave!

DAVE
(Shakes his head looking at Sam and knocks on the casket.)

Your family has some odd wedding traditions.
(Silence.)

ANNA
(Looking at Dave.)

You didn't do it right.

DAVE
(Shrugs.)

I didn't do what right?

SAM
(With frustration. Walks to the casket and knocks. Bum-ba-da-bum-bum. The women listen with rapt attention. Silence.)

Knock on the casket.
(Pauses.)
You didn't knock on the casket right.

DAVE
(With mild frustration.)

I didn't know there was a right way to knock on a casket.

CHRISTINA
(The women all look at each other without exchanging a word.)

We all heard it, right?

DAVE

Heard what?

SAM

Oh, never mind.
(Pauses.)
You're starting to look a whole lot better. Did they tell you how much longer it would be before your jacket was ready?

DAVE

They told me it would just be a couple of minutes.

SAM
(Pointing to the hallway.)
Why didn't you just stay there then?

DAVE

Well, they gave me these meal vouchers for the inconvenience.
(Distributes a menu and meal voucher to Sam, Anna, and Christina.)
And I wanted to see if you guys wanted something to eat.

ANNA
(Incredulously.)
Meal vouchers at a funeral home?

DAVE
(Nodding affirmatively.)
Oh yeah, today's special is veal parmesan with your choice of pasta as a side dish.

CHRISTINA
(Incredulously.)
They have a special of the day?

DAVE
(With mild disappointment.)

Yeah, it's too bad we didn't come yesterday.

                    SAM
             (Mutters under her breath.)
Well, that was poor planning on Great-Aunt Edna's part.

                CHRISTINA
            (Inquisitively. To Dave.)
Why?
                  (Pauses.)
What was the special yesterday?

                  DAVE
                (Shrugs.)
Yesterday was the all you can eat rib buffet.

                  ANNA
            (Incredulously.)
They have a buffet at a funeral home?

                  DAVE
                (Shrugs.)
Yeah, but that was yesterday.

                CARHOP
            (A carhop on roller skates carrying a tray of food rolls into the parlor. Looks around at those gathered.)
One special of the day with angel hair pasta?
            (The group remains silent. The carhop looks at an order form and realizes she is in the wrong parlor.)
Oh, I'm sorry.
            (Pauses.)
Wrong parlor.
            (Rolls out of the parlor toward the hallway.)

DAVE
(Pointing toward the hallway.)
See what I mean.

ANNA
(Shaking her head in disbelief.)
Is there a restaurant attached to the funeral parlor?

DAVE
(Pointing upward.)
Oh, no. The dining area is on the fourth floor.
(Moves his finger to the right, still pointing upward.)
Next to the IMAX Theater with stadium seating.

CHRISTINA
(Shaking her head in disbelief.)
There is an IMAX Theater in here too?

DAVE
(Nods in agreement.)
Oh yeah, they have first run movies too!

ANNA
(Shrugs.)
But why?

DAVE
(Shrugs.)
I'm not sure, but the place was packed.
(Motions his finger upward again.)
A lot of folks were hanging out in the cocktail lounge.

CHRISTINA
(Looking at Dave with disbelief.)
In this funeral home?

DAVE
(Motions to the group.)
Like I said, you guys should really check this place out.
(With a sense of reverence.)
It's an experience.

SAM
(Motions to Dave. With agitation.)
I'll give you an experience if you don't come back with your jacket in two minutes!

DAVE
(Pointing to the hallway.)
I'm on my way.

SAM
(Calls to Dave before he exits into the hallway.)
Oh Dave?

DAVE
(Turns his head to look at Sam.)
Yes, darling?

SAM
(With emphasis.)
The jacket.
(With increased emphasis.)
Only the jacket.

DAVE
(Dutifully.)
Yes, honey.

SAM
(With continued emphasis.)

No gelato.

No side trips for a snack.

No IMAX Theater.

No cocktail lounges.

(Dave nods in understanding.)

(Again, Dave nods in understanding.)

(Again, Dave nods in understanding.)

                    DAVE
(Timidly.)

I understand, honey.

(Pauses.)

Just the jacket.

(Dave exits into the hallway.)

                    ANNA
(Trying to sound supportive, looking at Sam.)

It's almost time for the wedding.

(Pauses.)

Are you getting excited?

                    SAM
(Shakes her hands, clearly feeling wedding jitters.)

I am.

(Pauses.)

Let's see what other pictures there are of Edna.

(Sam, Anna, and Christina walk toward the photo board. Sam stops to examine the photo board and singles out a photo. With excitement.)

Ah, here's a good one!

                CHRISTINA

Is that...?

           (Both Anna and Christina examine the photo that Sam is pointing to. Incredulously.)

           ANNA
           (With equal incredulity.)

The Beatles?

           SAM
           (Nodding affirmatively.)

The Fab Four adored Edna.

           ANNA
           (Stammers.)

How did she....

           (Pauses.)

When did she....

           CHRISTINA
           (Shaking her head in disbelief.)

Meet The Beatles?

           SAM
           (Nonchalantly.)
Oh, I think it was on one of her visits to see Elizabeth.

           CHRISTINA
           (Still shaking her head in disbelief.)

Queen Elizabeth?

           SAM
           (With enthusiasm.)

Exactly!

           (Lifts her finger in the air.)
The Beatles wanted to write a song for Edna.

ANNA
(In disbelief.)

They what?

SAM
(Nodding in affirmation.)

They did!
(Pauses.)
They wanted to name an entire album after Edna.

ANNA

They didn't do that, did they?

SAM
(Nodding negatively.)

Edna was too humble.
(Shrugs.)
Instead, they used an anagram for her name.

CHRISTINA
(With uncertainty.)

An anagram?

SAM
(Nodding in agreement.)

They scrambled some of the letters from her first, middle and last name and came up with Jude.
(Looking at Anna and Christina.)
Have you ever heard the song "Hey Jude"?

CHRISTINA
(In disbelief.)

Seriously?

SAM
(Nodding in agreement.)

Yeah!

(Pauses.)
That way they were able to write a song for Edna and name an album after her!

       ANNA
      (Still in disbelief.)
The Beatles?
      (Sam nods affirmatively.)
Wrote "Hey Jude" for your Great-Aunt Edna?

       SAM
      (Still nodding in agreement.)
That's what I was told.

       ANNA
      (Still in disbelief.)
I'll bet the Queen introduced Edna to other famous people as well.

       SAM
      (Nodding affirmatively.)
She did.

       ANNA
      (Pointing to the photo board.)
Are there pictures of any of them on the photo board?

       SAM
      (Scans the photo board.)
There is at least one more person that I know for sure.
      (Continuing to scan the photo board.)
Ah, here it is.
      (Points to a photo on the photo board.)

       ANNA
      (Anna and Christina examine the picture
      that Sam is pointing to.)
Who is that?

SAM
(Tapping the photo.)
Of course, it was before he became famous, but this is Gordon Ramsay.

CHRISTINA
(Joking.)
Are you going to tell us that Edna taught Gordon Ramsay how to cook?

SAM
(With excitement.)
Oh, so you already know?

CHRISTINA
(Anna and Christina shake their heads negatively.)
Just a lucky guess, I suppose.
(Mutters under her breath.)
Given everything else you said about Edna.

SAM
(Chuckles.)
Edna would always laugh when she told us.
(Laughs a bit.)
Gordon Ramsay couldn't even boil water before he met her.

ANNA
(In disbelief.)
Really?

CHRISTINA
(Mutters under her breath again.)
Does anything really surprise you at this point?

SAM

(Shrugs.)
Edna was quick to say that once she unleashed Gordon's talent, he took to cooking like a fish to water.

ANNA
(In disbelief.)
Wow.

SAM
(Nods affirmatively.)
Edna was very proud of Gordon Ramsay's success.

CHRISTINA
(Examining the photo board. Points to a photo.)
Who are these people with your Great-Aunt?

SAM
(Ponders for a moment.)
Hmm, let me think.
(With recollection.)
Oh, yeah! That's Edna with Mother Teresa and the Dali Lama.

ANNA
(Exchange glances of disbelief shaking their head negatively.)
How did Edna know Mother Teresa and the Dali Lama?

SAM
(Waxes.)
Oh, they really enjoyed each other's company.
(Pauses.)
They would see each other at least once a year.

CHRISTINA
Was it for spiritual direction?

ANNA

(Marvels.)
How fortunate to receive spiritual direction from both Mother Teresa and the Dali Lama.

SAM
(Nods negatively.)
Edna did not receive spiritual direction from them.

ANNA
(Questions.)
Yeah, but I thought you said they got together for spiritual direction.

SAM
(Nods affirmatively.)
Oh, absolutely!

ANNA
(Questions.)
You're not saying....

CHRISTINA
(Questions.)
Mother Teresa and the Dali Lama received spiritual direction from Edna?

SAM
(Nods affirmatively.)
Yup!
(Smiles.)
At least once a year.
(Points to the picture.)
Do you see how they are all smiling?

CHRISTINA
Yes.

SAM

(With satisfaction.)
You can tell this is after Mother Teresa and the Dali Lama received spiritual direction from Edna.
(Pauses.)
Before their contact with Edna they would both look so glum.

ANNA
(Points to a picture.)
What about this one?

SAM
(Tapping the photo.)
I forget exactly what Super Bowl that was, but it's a picture of Edna with Tom Brady.

CHRISTINA
(Shaking her head negatively.)
How did your Great-Aunt afford to go to the Super Bowl?
(Pauses.)
Did she have a lot of money?

SAM
(Shakes her head negatively.)
Oh no, Edna gave her money away to different charities.
(Pauses.)
Tom Brady invited her to the Super Bowl.
(Points to another photo.)
Just like this one.

ANNA
(Examines the picture.)
I see Edna in the picture.
(Pauses.)
But where is she at?

SAM
(Casually.)

That's Edna celebrating with the Houston Astros after their World Series victory.

CHRISTINA
(Shaking her head negatively.)
I'm guessing she was invited to attend the World Series, right?

SAM
(Nods in agreement.)
She was.
(Tapping the photo.)
That's the game where she threw out the first pitch.

ANNA
(Looking at Sam.)
Threw out the first pitch in a game of the World Series?

SAM
(Continuing to nod in agreement.)
The Houston Astros insisted.
(Pauses.)
They said it would bring them good luck!
(The sirens of fire trucks can be heard in the distance.

Anxiously looks at her wristwatch.)
Where is that man!

CHRISTINA
(Trying to distract Sam and calm her points to another picture.)
Oh, I didn't notice this picture before.

SAM
(Leans in to view the photo that Christina is pointing at.)
Oh, that one.

CHRISTINA
(Squinting at the picture.)
It kind of looks like Edna is holding a sledgehammer.
(Turns to Sam.)
Is that a sledgehammer?

SAM
(Nodding affirmatively.)
It is.

ANNA
(Also inspecting the picture. Looks at Sam.)
But why would she be holding a sledgehammer?

SAM
(Shrugs.)
Reagan insisted.

ANNA
(Inquisitively.)
Reagan?
(Sam nods affirmatively.)
Ronald Reagan?

SAM
(Continues to nod affirmatively.)
Yes.

CHRISTINA
(Looking at Sam.)
President Ronald Reagan?

SAM
(Continuing to nod affirmatively.)
Yes.

(Pauses.)
President Reagan demanded that Edna take the first swing to knock down the Berlin Wall.

CHRISTINA
(Inquisitively.)
The Berlin Wall?

SAM
(Continuing to nod affirmatively.)
Yes.
(Pauses.)
Gorbachev did not want the wall to come down.

ANNA
(Inquisitively.)
So, President Reagan wanted Edna to take the blame for knocking down the Berlin Wall?

SAM
(Nodding negatively.)
Oh, Heaven's no!
(Pauses.)
Reagan asked Gorbachev to take down the wall, and Gorbachev refused.
(Pauses.)
Although, once Gorbachev knew that Edna was going to take the first swing, it was only then that he agreed.

CHRISTINA
(Inquisitively.)
The Berlin Wall?
(Puzzled.)
In Germany?
(Still puzzled.)
Your Great-Aunt Edna?

SAM
(Nods affirmatively.)
That's the story that Edna told us!

DAVE
(Walks back into the parlor, in a clean white tuxedo. Holding something in his hands.)
Oh man!
(Pauses.)
Finally!

SAM
(Giving Dave a nod of approval.)
They did a great job cleaning your tuxedo, Dave!
(Looking at Dave's hands.)
What are you holding.
(Sternly.)
I hope it's not gelato!

DAVE
(Nods his head negatively.)
No gelato.
(Opens his hands to reveal what he is holding.)
They felt bad for me, so they gave me these from the gift shop.

ANNA
(In surprise.)
Gift shop?

CHRISTINA
(Looks at Anna.)
Would anything really surprise you at this point?

SAM
(Examining what is in Dave's hands.)

What are they?

                              DAVE
                            (With pride.)

Casket banks.

                              SAM

Casket what?

                              DAVE
                        (Still beaming with pride.)

They're little casket banks.
                        (Hands one to Sam, Anna and Christina holding one for himself.)

Look.
                        (Reaches into his pocket for a coin. Inserts a coin in the casket bank, and up pops the body inside the casket bank.)

The kids really seem to love them.

                              SAM
                        (Shaking her head.)

Maybe it takes the mind of a child to appreciate them!
                        (More sirens of fire trucks can be heard in the distance.

                        A person pushing a shopping cart pauses for a moment in the hallway in clear view of the audience. Dave points.)

                              DAVE

Do you see that guy there?

                              SAM
                        (The group turns their attention to the hallway.)

Yeah.

DAVE
I saw him up in the gift shop.
(Pauses.)
He really loaded up on the T-Shirts.

ANNA
T-Shirts?

DAVE
Yeah, the Funeral Home Mega-Plex T-Shirts.

CHRISTINA
Why would anyone want that?

DAVE
The T-Shirts have a lot of funny quotes on them.

ANNA
Funny quotes on the T-Shirts you buy in a funeral home?

DAVE
(Starts to chuckle.)
Oh yeah.
(Wipes his eye.)
Some of the quotes are hysterical.
(Pauses.)
Everyone in the gift shop was laughing.

ANNA
(Perplexed.)
Laughing in a funeral home?

DAVE
(Looks at the group.)
You guys really need to look around this place.
(Pauses.)

It has so much to offer.
                    (The person pushing the shopping cart moves out of view.)
There is a great selection of chocolates in the gift shop too.
                    (Pauses.)
There is also an entire section dedicated to….

                    CLOWN
                    (Before Dave can continue, a clown with big floppy shoes walks in and signs the guest book. Before leaving he turns to the group and says.)
Sorry for your loss.
                    (Collectively, the group nods in appreciation.

                    The clown notices how Sam and Dave are dressed. To Sam and Dave.)
Is this your wedding day?
                    (Sam and Dave nod affirmatively.)

                    SAM
                    (Smiles and shakes her head affirmatively.)
Yes, it is.

                    CLOWN
                    (Reaches into his pocket and pulls out several balloons. Starts to blow into the balloons. Pauses for a moment and says with excitement.)
I have just the thing for a bride and groom!
                    (Continues to blow up more balloons. With continued excitement. The group is watching the clown.)
You're going to love this!

          (Tries to form the balloons into a particular shape.)

You're not going to believe it!

          (Mangles the balloons together into a completely indescribable shape. With pride.)

A bride and groom balloon!

For the bride and groom!

          (Hands the mangled mess to Sam.)

DAVE
(Trying to sound excited and be polite.)

Wow, thanks!

CLOWN
(Still full of pride.)

No worries.

          (Bows his head.)

Once again, I'm sorry for your loss.

          (Makes his way to the hallway. The sound of the clown's floppy shoes can be heard after he exits.)

SAM
(Turning the balloons at various angles examines the balloons.)

A bride and groom?

ANNA
(Looking at the balloons.)

It kind of looks like Dave.

CHRISTINA
(Looking at the balloons.)

Oh, yeah! I can see it!

DAVE

(Looking at the balloons.)
It looks like me?

                  ANNA
                  (Nodding in agreement. To Dave.)
It must be like looking into a mirror.

                  CHRISTINA
                  (Nodding in agreement.)
An uncanny resemblance!

                  DAVE
                  (Not aware he is being mocked.)
Maybe, I'm looking at it from the wrong angle.

                  ANNA
                  (Acting as if she is admiring the balloons.)
A very handsome groom, indeed.

                  CHRISTINA
                  (Nodding in agreement.)
Oh yes, a very handsome groom.

                  DAVE
                  (Struggling to discern a shape.)
Really?

                  SAM
                  (Finds a trash container and unceremoniously dumps the balloons into the container.)
I think I'll leave this little treasure right here.
                  (Looks at the group.)
I think we're finally ready to leave.

                  ELIZABETH

(Runs into the parlor and gives Sam a hug.)

Oh, thank God, you're here.

SAM
(Surprised.)

Mom, what are you doing here?
(Perplexed.)
Shouldn't we all be heading to the church?

ELIZABETH
(Shakes her head negatively.)

Oh, you didn't hear?

SAM
(Stunned.)

Hear what?

ELIZABETH
(Struggling not to get emotional.)

The church caught fire.

SAM
(Everyone gasps.)

What?

ANNA
(Trying to calm Sam.)

Don't worry Sam, we'll get through this.

ELIZABETH
(Also trying to be consoling.)

That's right, Sam.
(Pauses.)
We'll get through this.

DAVE

> (Embraces Sam.)

It will be okay, honey.

> CHRISTINA
> (To Sam.)

Focus on the positives, we're all safe.

> SAM
> (Shaking her head in disbelief.)

This can't be happening.

> (Points to the casket.)

First, Edna, and now this?

> DAVE
> (Continues to console Sam.)

Like Christina said, we're all safe.
> (Pauses.)

We'll find another place to get married.

> SAM
> (Looking at the group. Clearly in shock.)

But the flowers.

> ANNA
> (Trying to be consoling.)

You don't need flowers to get married.

> CHRISTINA
> (Also trying to be consoling.)

That's right Sam. It's not about the place or the flowers.

> DAVE
> (Dave's phone rings. Before answering the phone, he looks to see who is calling him. An indistinct voice can be heard on the phone talking to Dave.)

Yes, pastor?
          (Nodding.)
That's right. That's right.
          (Continuing to nod.)
Everyone is fine, we're at the funeral home down the road.
          (Continuing to nod.)
Yes, the Mega-Plex.
          (Continuing to nod.)
Oh, you were going to come here later for the daily special.
          (Pauses.)
That's right, today's special is veal parmesan with the side pasta.
          (Pauses.)
Oh really? You were here yesterday as well for the buffet?
          (Pauses.)
Oh my, that sounds amazing.
          (Nods.)
Oh, we're in the parlor for Ed....
          (Nods.)
Yes, Edna Murphy. Yes, she was an amazing person, pastor.
          (Listens for many seconds. Dave continues to nod and say "yes" several times as he listens.)
Yes, she was exceptional. You'll find her parlor if you look for....
          (Nods.)
Okay, so you know about the neon signs.
          (Nods.)
Yes, pastor, you're right. The signs are impossible to miss.
          (Questions.)
Here? Sure, that's fine with me. I'll ask Sam and see what she thinks.
          (Pauses.)
Okay, we'll see you in a few minutes.

          SAM
          (Looking at Dave.)
The pastor is coming here?

          DAVE

(Nods.)

Yes.

(Pauses.)

It sounds like he is very familiar with this place.

(Clears his throat.)

And with Edna.

ELIZABETH
(Nods in agreement.)

I'm not surprised.

(Looking at the group.)

The pastor and Edna went skydiving together many times.

SAM
(Asking Dave.)

What did the pastor want you to ask me?

DAVE
(Hesitantly.)

Well….

SAM

Yes?

DAVE
(Reluctantly.)

The pastor mentioned that the church was burned to the ground and perhaps….

SAM

Yes?

ELIZABETH
(A little agitated.)

Spit it out, Dave!

DAVE

(Glares at Elizabeth.)
The pastor wanted to know if we would consider getting married here.

SAM

In a funeral home?

DAVE
(Motioning to the casket.)
This way Great-Aunt Edna will be a part of the celebration too.

ANNA
(Looking at Sam.)

It's not a bad idea, Sam.

CHRISTINA
(To Sam.)

The place isn't important.
(Pauses.)
Anna and I can call the wedding guests and let them know about the change of venue.

DAVE
(To Sam.)

It's entirely up to you, Sam.

SAM
(Contemplates.)

Getting married in a funeral home is not what I imagined I would do when I was a little girl, but
(Pauses.)
given the circumstances.
(Hesitates.)
Why not.

ANNA
(Looking at Sam.)

Christina and I will go and call the guests to let them know of the change.

                    CHRISTINA
                    (Nods to Sam.)

We'll take care of this, Sam. Don't worry.
                    (Anna and Christina quickly walk to the hallway.)

                    MR. WESLEY
                    (Enters the parlor. Addresses Sam and Dave.)

Your pastor just called me and said that there may be a wedding here.

                    SAM
                    (Nods in agreement.)

You don't mind?
                    (Cautiously.)

Do you?

                    MR. WESLEY
                    (Shakes his head negatively.)

Heavens no!
                    (Pointing off stage.)

I understand the church burned to the ground, so....
                    (Trying to sound consoling.)

We understand completely.

                    SAM
                    (Gratefully.)

Thank you so much, sir.

                    MR. WESLEY
                    (Trying to imbue confidence.)

Everything will be fine.
                    (Looking to Dave.)

Right lad?

DAVE
(Nodding in agreement.)
Yes, sir.

MR. WESLEY
(Kindly.)
We can accommodate a larger gathering if you would like to use the chapel.
(Pointing to the casket.)
Of course, Edna is welcome to attend.

SAM
(Looking around the funeral parlor.)
We may need to do that.

MR. WESLEY
(Confidently.)
No worries!
(Patting Sam on the hand.)
I'll make sure the staff prepares the chapel for the wedding.
(Pauses.)
We can also bring the floral arrangements to the chapel.

DAVE
Thank you, sir.

MR. WESLEY
Not a problem.
(Pointing above him.)
As you may know, we also have dining facilities.

DAVE
Yes, I saw them.
(Pauses.)
They are amazing.

MR. WESLEY

Did you also notice the ballroom?

DAVE

Ballroom?

MR. WESLEY
(With pride.)

Oh, yes sir.
    (Motions with his hand.)
It's right next to the concert hall.

ELIZABETH
(Somewhat sarcastically.)

The next thing you're going to tell me is that there is a casino in this funeral home.

MR. WESLEY
(Apologetically.)

Not yet, Ma'am.
    (Shrugs.)
Although, the construction for that is under way.

ELIZABETH
(Incredulously.)

As a part of this funeral home?

MR. WESLEY
(With pride.)

Absolutely!
    (Nodding affirmatively.)
We need to maintain our Mega-Plex status.

SAM
(Timidly.)

Sir?

MR. WESLEY
(In an empathetic voice.)
Yes, Ma'am.

SAM
(Shyly.)
Is there any chance we can have the wedding catered here?

MR. WESLEY
(Cheerfully.)
You're in luck!
(Pauses.)
The dining facilities are not booked for an event today. So, the dining facility is at your disposal.

SAM
(With a sense of gratitude and relief.)
Oh, thank you!

MR. WESLEY
(Inclines his hand toward Sam's ear.)
We have a full menu, I assure you.

DAVE
(Meekly.)
I hate to impose further, but….

MR. WESLEY
(In an empathetic voice.)
Yes, sir.

DAVE
(Cautiously asks.)
Would the ballroom also be available?

MR. WESLEY
(Cheerfully.)

It is sir!
                    (Pauses.)
I'll see to it myself that the ballroom is prepared for your reception.

                         DAVE
                    (Gratefully.)
Thank you, sir!

                         MR. WESLEY
                    (Cheerfully.)
Of course, sir!

                         DAVE
                    (To Mr. Wesley.)
Could we pay you after the wedding?

                         MR. WESLEY
                    (Inquisitively.)
Pay me?

                         DAVE
Yes, for the chapel, dining hall, and ballroom.

                         MR. WESLEY
                    (Nods his head negatively.)
Sir, the bill has already been paid.

                         DAVE
                    (Inquisitively.)
Paid? Who would have done that?

                         MR. WESLEY
                    (Points toward the casket.)
Edna paid for the wedding earlier.
                    (Motions with his hand.)
The chapel, dining hall and ballroom.
                    (With emphasis.)

She even included gratuities!

>   DAVE
>   (Stunned.)

How is that possible?

>   MR. WESLEY
>   (Nodding his head negatively.)

I don't know, sir, but Edna was a truly remarkable person.

>   ELIZABETH
>   (To Sam.)

It's all going to work out, dear.

>   SAM
>   (Confidently.)

It is!

>   ELIZABETH
>   (Pointing over to the casket.)

Edna pulled some strings for you.
>   (Somewhat emotionally.)

She had a way of doing that.

>   SAM
>   (With melancholy.)

I wish I had gotten to know her better.

>   ELIZABETH
>   (Nodding in affirmation.)

She was one of a kind!
>   (Starts to chuckle.)

Did you ever hear the story of how Edna stopped a bank robbery?

>   SAM
>   (Surprised.)

She what?

ELIZABETH
(Nodding in affirmation.)

Really!

(Still chuckling.)

She put the bank robber in a full Nelson.

(Pauses.)

The story was in all the local papers.

SAM
(Inquisitively.)

Was that a long time ago?

ELIZABETH
(Nodding negatively.)

No, that was last week.

DAVE
(The pastor walks into the parlor with his suit jacket smoking. Without hesitation Mr. Wesley takes the flowers out of a small floral arrangement and splashes the water on the pastor's jacket to extinguish the smoke.

Cocks his head looking at Mr. Wesley and exclaims.)

Why didn't you splash him with chocolate milk?

(Blackout. End of play. Curtain.)

Into The Machine

A Play in Two Acts

Copyright © 2005   E-mail: profjim@email.com

Cast of Characters

KRIS – Tall man with a muscular build in his late thirties. Kris has black hair and a clean shaven ruggedly handsome face.

DAN – Sharp witted, eccentric, stocky man in his early fifties is quick to find the humor in a situation. Dan has light brown hair, wears glasses and is a free thinker.

DR. HAMILTON – Tall man in his mid-fifties with a piercing glance. Dr. Hamilton is decisive, opinionated and to the point. Dr. Hamilton will often use his hands when making a point. Dr. Hamilton is wearing a dark suit, white shirt, and a light grey tie.

DAVID – Tall middle-aged man with short, cropped hair and dower demeanor. David speaks in punctuated sentences and often looks over his eyeglasses in a demeaning manner. David is wearing a dark suit, a white shirt, and a red tie.

LARRY – Older soft-spoken gentleman. Larry has a receding hairline and salt and pepper hair. Larry wears horn-rimmed glasses, suspenders, a crisply pressed dress shirt and a conservatively patterned tie.

ZIA – A strikingly beautiful woman in her mid-twenties with a charismatic smile. Zia has almond shaped brown eyes, full luscious lips and thick, straight brunette hair that flows onto her back.

Act I Scene 1

(In a computer lab Dan is standing beside Kris who is sitting in an elaborate contraption that looks somewhat like a dentist chair. Kris is holding a handheld electronic device which is hooked up to a computer via a tangle of wires that encircles him.

The lab has a variety of computers and monitors. There is also a small table with a couple of chairs off to the left side of the stage.

In this scene:
Dan and Kris)

DAN
(With a twinkle in his eye looking at Kris)

Comfortable?

KRIS

Huh?

DAN
(Chuckles)
I was just wondering if you were comfortable.

KRIS
(Smiles)

Absolutely!
(Looking at the tangle of wires that surrounds him)
I've never been more comfortable in my life. Although,
(Pauses)

can I make a request?

DAN
Sure!

KRIS
Will you fluff my pillow?

DAN
(Starts to laugh)
Just a minute. Let me call the concierge.
(Smiles)
While we're waiting for the concierge to show up, let's run through this one more time. Okay?

KRIS
Sounds good to me.

DAN
Tell 'ya what, you explain it to me, so I know that you understand it. Okay?

KRIS
You've got it boss.
(Pauses)
Hmm, let's see where should I start?
(Clears his throat)
Well, let me start with the purpose of this experiment.

DAN
That works.

KRIS
(Able to point with limited mobility because of the wires attached.)
In a nutshell, what we're trying to do is to get me
(Pointing to himself)

into that computer
                (Pointing to a computer a couple of feet away)
over there.

                DAN

Bingo!

                KRIS

Or should I state it more clearly by saying that we are trying to
                (Puts emphasis on the word "painlessly")
painlessly get me into that computer.

                DAN
                (Shaking his head negatively and smiling)
Painless is such a nebulous term.

                KRIS

Not if I'm the one experiencing the pain!

                DAN
                (Nodding in agreement)
Okay. Okay. So, we're trying to
                (Puts emphasis on the word "painlessly")
painlessly get you into the computer.
                (Muttering under his breath)
Kinda takes the fun out of it if you ask me.

                KRIS

What was that?

                DAN

Nothing.
                (Smiling)

Nothing at all.

KRIS
Why am I starting to have second thoughts about this experiment?

DAN
(Jovially)
Come on, kid, I'm playing with you.
(Kris gives Dan a suspicious look. Pointing to himself)
Do you think that I
(Pointing to Kris)
would inflict pain on you?

KRIS
(Looks at the tangle of wires that surround him. Clears his throat, cocks his head as best he can given his limited mobility, and looks squarely at Dan.)
Let me continue.
(Dan shrugs his shoulders as if he is stunned by Kris' response)
We're trying to get me into that computer by way of this remarkable contraption that you put together.

DAN
(Nodding in appreciation)
It is kinda remarkable, isn't it?

KRIS
(Emphatically)
Yeah! Remarkable that you talked me into being the first micro voyager.

DAN
(Patting his belly)
Well, kid, I'm afraid that I might not have fit as well as you.

KRIS
Oh good, so I'm going to be cramped and confined in the computer, eh?

DAN
(Shrugs)
Well, it kinda depends on your definition of....

KRIS
No, Dan, seriously, do you think I have anything to worry about?

DAN
(Reassuringly)
Not at all.
(Shaking his head negatively and looking Kris in the eyes)
Believe me, Kris, there's no way that I'd put you into a dangerous situation.
(Pointing to the device in Kris' hand)
Besides, don't forget about the features on your handheld control unit.

KRIS
(Bends his neck to look at the control unit)
Oh, yeah, that's right, so let me talk about the control unit.
(Pauses)
Hmm, there are quite a few things I can say about the control unit.

DAN
(Nodding in agreement)
Yup.

KRIS
First off, when I use the control unit there are several aspects of the computer that I can monitor.
(Pauses)

There is one thing though.

DAN

What's that?

KRIS

Sitting like this, it's kinda hard to see the controls on the unit.

DAN

Sure, right now, but once I put on the virtual reality helmet on your head
> (Pointing to a device which is currently dangling below the head section in the chair that Kris is sitting in)

it will be just like you were standing up, and the control unit will be in clear view.

KRIS
> (Gives Dan a skeptical glance)

Have you tested any of this equipment?

DAN

Well, that's kinda what we're doing now.

KRIS
> (Sounding a little concerned)

Using me to test the equipment?

DAN

I'm not going to lie to you, kid. This has never been done before.
> (Pauses)

Look, if you feel uncomfortable doing this, then we'll stop now.
> (Pauses)

No hard feelings.

KRIS

Well, I knew that this was untested to some degree.

(Pauses)
I guess I wasn't aware that the whole thing was untested.

DAN

The electronic components are all solid.
(Pauses)
The virtual journey into a computer hasn't been done before.
(Shrugs)
That's the new part.

KRIS

So, I'm not going to physically be in the computer?

DAN
(Emphatically)

No, no, not at all.
(Shaking his head negatively)
Only virtually.

KRIS

Okay, for some reason I thought that I would physically be in the computer.

DAN

It should feel as though you're physically in the computer; although, you'll physically be safe and sound here in the lab.

KRIS

Ah, now it makes sense.
(Pauses)
Actually, I do remember talking to you about this last week, and you did mention the virtual reality helmet would make it feel as though I was physically inside the computer.

DAN

Exactly! That's what we're going to put to the test today.

KRIS
(Nodding affirmatively)
Okay, okay, so, let me continue with how all this stuff works.

DAN

I'm all ears.

KRIS

Once I put on the virtual reality helmet, I'll be able to clearly see this handheld control device.

DAN
(Nodding in agreement)

Right.

KRIS
(Tilts up the electronic handheld device so that he can see it better)

And, on this little gizmo there are several controls.
(Dan nods in agreement)
A couple of the primary ones are the communication controls that we will use to keep in touch.

DAN
(Continuing to nod affirmatively)

That's right.
(Pointing to a monitor a few feet away)
I will be able to see everything you type with your handheld device on my command console, and everything I type at the command console you will be able to read on your handheld. Make sense?

KRIS

Sure.
(Pauses)
So, if there is a problem on either end we can communicate with one another.

DAN

Exactly!

KRIS

And, since I am going into the computer to diagnose problems, there are several controls that I can use for that such as a network view, a....

DAN
(Prompting Kris for an answer)

And the network view will show you....

KRIS

The network view will show me the communication on the network.

DAN
(Puts emphasis on the word "only")

Only the communication on the network.

KRIS
(Nods in agreement)

Right! Only the communication on the network, just as the software view will show me
(Puts emphasis on the word "only")
only the software running, the hardware view will show me only the hardware, and the physical view will show me only the physical connections to the computer.
(Pauses)

And oh yeah.

DAN

What?

KRIS

I almost forgot to mention two of the most important buttons.
(Pauses)

The engage and the disengage button.

DAN

Yeah, those are kinda helpful.

KRIS

Once you put that virtual reality helmet on my head, I start the process by pressing the
          (Puts emphasis on the word "engage")
engage button.
          (Pauses)
Then, when I'm done wandering around inside of the computer and I want to exit, I press the
          (Puts emphasis on the word "disengage")
disengage button.

DAN

It sounds like you've got it!

KRIS

The way you designed it is very intuitive, so I really don't think I'll have any problems.

DAN

And, if you do, we can always communicate with one another.

KRIS

Sure! Believe me if there is a nasty virus chasing me, you'll be the first to know.

DAN

Again, you'll only be there virtually, so there is no way that you can get hurt.

KRIS

Is that what it says in the owner's manual for this contraption?

DAN
(Shrugs)
I don't know.
(Pauses)
I haven't written the owner's manual yet.

KRIS
Maybe you can start on it while I go on my little excursion.

DAN
I'll be monitoring your vital signs while you're on your excursion.
(Lifts his finger in the air)
But I'll get around to writing it one day.

KRIS
Dan, I can see you creating a machine like this that will allow a person to virtually go inside a computer, although
(Pauses)
I'm not sure that I can see you taking the time to document the process.

DAN
(Shrugs)
Kris, if this ends up being a success, then we can hire a person to write the documentation for us.

KRIS
Why not? Just think of the computer problems we can solve with your contraption.

DAN
Oh, that reminds me.

KRIS
Here we go.

(Pauses)
Reminds you of what?

DAN
There is at least one problem with the computer that I am aware of.
(Pauses)
I'm anxious to see if you can find it.

KRIS
I'll do my best, and let you know once I come out of the computer.

DAN
So, do you think you're ready
(Motions with his hand)
to give it a whirl?

KRIS
I'm as ready as I'll ever be.

DAN
(Walks over and picks up the VR helmet)
Do you want me to put the virtual reality helmet on?

KRIS
I guess I should say something profound first, huh?

DAN
Okay, Neil Armstrong, go ahead.

KRIS
(Chuckles)
Put the damn helmet on.

DAN
That's it?

KRIS
What?

DAN
Your profound statement?
(Shrugs)
That's it?

KRIS
The best I can do on short notice.

DAN
Good luck, Kris, I envy you.

KRIS
I know you do, Dan.
(Pauses)
Thanks for giving me the opportunity.
(Dan starts to put the VR helmet on Kris)
Dan?

DAN
(Holds the VR helmet in his hands)

Yes?

KRIS
I'll still be able to hear you after you put the virtual reality helmet on, right?

DAN
You'll be able to hear me until the time when you press the engage button.

KRIS
What if nothing happens after I press the engage button?

                    DAN

Well, then we'll head off to the bar, get a couple beers, and I'll figure out what went wrong.

                    KRIS

Sounds like a plan.

                    DAN
          (Still holding the VR helmet)
Are you ready?

                    KRIS

I'm ready.

                    DAN
          (Starts to put the VR helmet on Kris)
Okay. I'm starting to put the virtual reality helmet on you.
          (Carefully places the VR helmet over Kris's head)
Once the virtual reality helmet is on you, the first thing you will see is the handheld device.

                    KRIS

I see it.
          (Somewhat excitedly)
Dan, I see it.

                    DAN

Okay, my friend, I'll stay here and monitor your vital signs.
          (Pauses)
Let me know before you press the engage button, okay?

                    KRIS

Let me get familiar with the virtual reality helmet.
          (Pauses)
This thing is pretty cool.
          (Pauses)

I'll say the word "engage" just before I press the button.
>(Clears his throat)

I'll engage in three seconds.
>(Starts a countdown)

Three. Two. One. Engage!

DAN
>(Directs his attention to the display panels monitoring Kris's vital signs.)

So far, so good.

>(Nodding contently. Three seconds later he is puzzled and peers intently at the command console)

What's all this?

KRIS
>(Ten seconds after he entered into the computer he returns)

Dan?

>(Pauses)

Dan, are you still here?

DAN

I'm here, Kris.

>(Walks over to Kris)

Was there a problem?

>(Pointing to the command console)

The command console started to flood with communication information.

KRIS
>(Clearly very excited)

That was wild!

>(Pauses)

Man, I'm sorry I took so long, but

                        (Still excited, puts emphasis on the word "that")

that was wild!

                                DAN
                             (Puzzled)

What? What was wild?

                                  KRIS

The whole thing!

                        (Still very excited, Dan walks over and takes the VR helmet off of Kris)

Whoo hooo! You've got to try this thing.

                                  DAN

But Kris you were just gone for a couple of seconds.

                                  KRIS

Check the logs.
                        (Pointing over to the control console)

I wrote down everything,
                        (Trying to catch his breath)

it should all be recorded in the logs.

                                  DAN
                        (Walks toward the command console)

So, how long do you think you were gone?

                                  KRIS
                        (Breathing starts to return to normal)

I don't know.
                        (Pauses)

I'd guess maybe four hours,
                        (Shrugs)

maybe five hours. I don't know for sure, but I was gone for a while.

DAN
(Looking at the command console, shaking his head in disbelief putting emphasis on the word "is".)

This *is* wild.

KRIS

See, it's all there.

DAN
(Prints the logs to the printer)

You found the issue that I planted....

KRIS

Oh, that computer program that was looping.
(Nods)
Yeah, that was the first thing that I checked out.
(Pauses)
I figured that was the issue you planted.

DAN
(Still looking at the console walks back towards Kris)

Here, let me get you disconnected from all these wires.
(Pauses)
I've got so many questions to ask you.

KRIS
(Still excited)

Okay, okay.
(Pauses)
I'm telling you, Dan, you've got to try this.
(Dan works at getting Kris disconnected)
You're a genius, my friend.
(Exclaims)
A genius!

DAN
Well, don't break your arm patting me on the back, because I have to confess, I'm a little puzzled.

KRIS
About what?

DAN
    (Kris is now free from the tangle of wires and stands up from the chair.)
I assumed that there would be a time difference, but I never assumed that the time difference would be so extreme.

KRIS
Hey, I'm only guessing.
    (Nodding)
Although it sure did seem like I was gone for at least four hours.
    (Shakes his head)
You have no idea how much I did while I was away.

DAN
    (Pointing to the command console)
Oh, I can gather.
    (Puts his hands on Kris' shoulders)
You've gotta tell me what you saw in there.

KRIS
    (Shakes his head)
Oh, where do I begin?

DAN
    (Motions over to the table in the lab)
Let's go sit at the table.
    (Walks to the printer to retrieve the pages he printed)
I just want to pick up a hard copy of the logs you entered.

(Dan walks to the table as Kris sits down at the table.)

So, how did you identify so many problems with the computer?

KRIS
(Dan sits beside Kris)

Dan,

(Looking Dan in the eyes)

it was easy. I mean, I could see the problems.

DAN

What do you mean, you could see the problems?

KRIS

Well, first of all when I entered the computer, I zoomed all the way out with the handheld unit, and then off in the distance, I saw some activity that attracted my attention, so I walked to that area and saw a frenzy of activity.

(Shakes his head)

I wasn't quite sure what to do next to identify the problem, so I zoomed in a little to try and get a closer look.

DAN
(Intently listening)

Okay.

KRIS

So, as I zoom in, I get greater and greater detail, until….

DAN
(Softly)

Yes?

KRIS

I zoom in so much and I see these shiny blue, faceless robots.
(Thinking)

Gee, I don't know what to call them. They all look completely identical to one another, kinda like smooth, human-sized, robots in a way. Of course, size really has no meaning.

DAN
(Questioning)
Robots?

KRIS
Yeah, I mean,
(Pauses)
it's kinda hard to describe these, these
(Pauses)
automatons are all scurrying about going off in different directions.

DAN
So, what would these
(Tentatively says the word "automatons")
automatons do?

KRIS
These automatons would perform the functions inside the computer.
(Motions with his hand)
Moving without interruption and with purpose, these nameless automatons would keep moving to perform the tasks that they were programmed to accomplish.
(Pauses)
I'll call them automatons, okay?

DAN
(Uncertain)
Okay.

KRIS
These automatons are there going around, and around and around.
(Pauses)

Well, to be honest, it looked a little odd to me, so I ask one of the automatons why they're doing the same action over and over again.

DAN
Did the automaton answer you?

KRIS
No, but the automaton did show me something.

DAN
What?

KRIS
The automaton stopped and showed me the code that it was following to perform the same repetitive task.
    (Gestures with his hand)
Now, I used to program before.

DAN
    (Nodding)
Of course.

KRIS
So, I was able to interpret the code that the automaton showed me, and when I looked at the code the automaton showed me I saw that you were the author of the code, and based on the comments you put in the code
    (Shakes his finger at Dan as if scolding him)
you intentionally inserted an infinite loop into the program.

DAN
    (Gasps)
Yes, I did.

KRIS
So, once I discovered that problem, I logged the issue.

                    DAN
Did you have the ability to correct the issue?

                    KRIS
              (Shakes his head negatively)
No. the automaton would not allow me to modify the code; although, the automatons did share the code with me so that I could identify the problem.

                    DAN
                 (Incredulous)
Amazing!

                    KRIS
Oh, that's just the beginning.

                    DAN
                (Encouragingly)
Go on.

                    KRIS
Since I was inside the computer...
              (Points to the computer across the room. Excitedly.)
Dan, I was in the computer!

                    DAN
                (Shakes his head)
This is amazing.
                    (Pauses)
Go on, Kris.

                    KRIS
            (Shaking his head in disbelief)
You know I still can't believe it but let me go on.

DAN

Okay.

KRIS

So, since I was already in the computer I figured that I would look around and see if there were any other issues that I could identify.

DAN
(Softly)

Sure.

KRIS

So, after identifying the first problem, I zoom all the way out with the software view, and don't really see anything of any consequence.

DAN

But you did see other software issues?

KRIS

Yeah, I did see a couple of problems with some of the applications running,
        (Shrugs)
and I did check them out; although, I guess I would classify them as software tuning issues.
        (Pointing to the hard copy in front of Dan)
I recorded the information in the log.

DAN
(Slides his glasses on and looks at the printout for a while)

I see. I see.
        (Pauses)
You even found some issues with the operating system, for crying out loud.

                             KRIS
                           (Nodding)
Oh yeah, that's true.
                           (Excitedly)
Oh!

                             DAN
Yeah?

                             KRIS
There was one firmware issue that I encountered that was kind of interesting.

                             DAN
Tell me about it.

                             KRIS
Well, again, the way I generally found the significant issues was when I was zoomed out completely.

                             DAN
Okay.

                             KRIS
So, I see some activity, and it looked,
                      (Looking at Dan intently)
I mean it looked like the automatons were carrying blue square things with them, and one by one they were turned away when they came to a certain place.

                             DAN
Turned away?

                             KRIS
Yeah, they were redirected by this other automaton who only accepted automatons carrying green squares.

DAN
Huh?

KRIS
Yeah, I was a little curious, so I go and ask the automaton that was directing the traffic, why he didn't accept the blue squares.

DAN
What did you find out?

KRIS
Well, pretty much in the same fashion, the automaton revealed to me the code that drove the decision process.

DAN
What did you find this time?

KRIS
The code showed that it would only accept one condition, but not both.

DAN
How did you know that it was a firmware issue?

KRIS
Well, a couple of things.
(Dan nods in anticipation)
First off, I saw this activity after I used the hardware view to investigate a certain chip on the motherboard.

DAN
Oh, okay.
(Looking at Kris)
So, you knew that you were in a specific chip?

KRIS
Exactly!

> (Pointing over to the chair where he took his micro voyage)

That handheld device is really cool, you can be in the hardware view, and while you're in the hardware view you can check out the software, physical connections, and so on

> (Emphatically)

within each view!

> (Shakes his head)

It's very cool!

DAN
> (Shaking his head looking at the hard copy)

This is amazing.

> (Looks up and looks at Kris)

And you did a great job recording all of the issues.

KRIS

Thanks.

> (Pauses)

Do you want to read the rest of the logs?

DAN

No, no, I want to hear what else you found.

KRIS
> (Pointing to the hard copy)

In the logs I tried to categorize each kind of problem.

DAN
> (Nodding)

I like the way you wrote this down.

> (Pauses)

It makes it very easy to fix the problems after you read the description of what you wrote.

> (Looking at Kris)

Please continue.

                    KRIS
Okay,
                    (Shakes his head)
Whew, Dan, I tell you, I'm still on a high from this experience, it was amazing.

                    DAN
                    (With a smile on his face)
I guess we can call this a success?

                    KRIS
                    (Emphatically)
A complete success!
                    (Pauses)
Okay, let me tell you what I did next.

                    DAN
Okay.

                    KRIS
So, I continue to check out the different views to see how many problems I can identify.

                    DAN
                    (Nodding affirmatively)
Makes sense.
                    (Pointing to the hardcopy)
Oh, what's this one?

                    KRIS
                    (Peering to see which item Dan is pointing at)
Which one?

                    DAN
The one you have here about a

(Questioning)
a power cord?

KRIS
(Nodding affirmatively)
Oh that.
(Pointing over to the computer)
Yeah, you might want to consider replacing the power cord on the second power supply.

DAN
Huh?

KRIS
Well, I was in the physical view, and I thought.
(Shrugs)
what the heck, so I continued my journey into the power cable.

DAN
(Gasps)
Amazing!

KRIS
To me, it was all connected,
(Pauses)
just like following a road. It was all connected.

DAN
So, how could you tell that one power cable was bad?

KRIS
Well, I went through both power cables, and
(Pauses)
when I went through one of the cables, and when I zoomed in, I could see that every once in a while the automatons would bump into each other, crackle and then disappear.

                    DAN
            (Gasps and then softly says)
You were at the atomic level.

                    KRIS
            (Smiles)
That's what I call zooming in.

                    DAN
            (Shaking his head in disbelief)
You were looking at individual electrons,
            (Pauses)
which, for purposes of comprehension appeared to look like automatons.

                    KRIS
            (Pointing to the chair in the middle of
            the stage)
Hey, I'm telling you Dan, you've got to check this thing out.
            (Reverently looking at Dan and puts
            emphasis on the word "are".)
You *are* a genius! You should get a Nobel Prize for this.

                    DAN
            (Shaking his head)
Think about the possible applications of this technology.
            (Gestures with his hand)
I mean, if you can also go into the power cable, this experiment
            (Pauses)
this experiment exceeded my wildest expectations!

                    KRIS
Dan, walking into the power cable was just like walking down a street.

                    DAN
Do you have any idea how far you could have gone?

                            KRIS
It seemed like I could have kept on walking forever.
                       (Shakes his head)
I'm telling you; this was amazing.
                            (Pauses)
The cool part of it too.

                             DAN
The cool part of it was that I could zoom out to see the
                       (Opens his arms)
big picture, or I could zoom in to see
                            (Puts his hands together. Emphatically,
                            emphasizing the word "very")
very granular details. Let me give you an example.
                       (Ponders for a second)
Oh, look at my entry for the I/O issue.

                             DAN
                    (Looking at the hard copy of the logs)
Let me find it.

                            KRIS
                    (Also looking at the hard copy)
Maybe it's on the next page.
                       (Dan flips the page)
Oh yeah, here it is.
                       (Pointing to a spot on the page)

                             DAN
Oh, okay, the I/O channels.

                            KRIS
Right.

                             DAN

     (Glances at the entry in the log, then
     looks over to Kris and nods)
Okay.

       KRIS
So, I'm walking around in the computer and by and large everything seems to be working just fine,
     (Dan nods encouraging him to continue)
but off in the distance, I see some cluster of activity that seems as though it may be a potential problem.

       DAN
     (Softly)
Okay.

       KRIS
     (Exclaims)
Oh, and I should mention that I'm still zoomed out.
     (Dan nods)
So, I approach the area of interest,
     (Shrugs)
I guess the closest thing that I could compare it to would be to say that so far I have seen the situation as if I was in a helicopter looking down on streets and buildings.

       DAN
     (Nods)
Gotcha.

       KRIS
Then, once I was over the area of interest, I zoomed in, and
     (Shrugs)
I guess you can say that was like going from the helicopter view onto the street, or inside the building.

       DAN
     (Tentatively)

Okay.

KRIS
Let's say I see something at the building level.

DAN
Okay.

KRIS
I know that there is something of interest in the building, but I don't know quite yet which floor, or which room.
(Dan continues to nod)
I continue investigating, and zooming in until I finally arrive in a specific room, if
(Pauses)
you want to call it that.

DAN
No, that kinda makes sense.
(Nods)
That's a great analogy.

KRIS
Also, if there was something of interest at the street level view, I would continue walking until I came to the specific area that attracted my attention.

DAN
Oh, I see.

KRIS
So, in this case, I see this swirl of activity in front of me with a bunch of automatons trying to get across a bridge,
(Pauses)
and as it turned out, I could see the automatons that wanted to cross the bridge far outnumbered the automatons who were able to cross the bridge.

(Pauses)
Every so often I would see an automaton falling off the bridge.

DAN
Did you ever feel as though you were in danger?

KRIS
No, even though I could interact with the automatons when I asked them questions, it was like I was watching the whole thing from behind a camera lens.
(Shakes his head)
I never once felt as though I was in danger.

DAN
So, what made you come to the conclusion that this was a problem with not enough I/O channels?

KRIS
Well, again, I stopped and asked an automaton why it was waiting in line, and why from time to time one would fall off the bridge.

DAN
And what did the automaton say?

KRIS
Well, the automatons never actually spoke to me.

DAN
(Apologetically)
Oh, that's right, you mentioned that before.

KRIS
No, no, that's a good question, but I do want to clarify that the automatons never actually spoke to me, they communicated with me by either showing me the code instructions that they were following, or in this case, showing me the configuration that they were following.

                    DAN
So, the automaton showed you the connection between the computer and the storage area network?

                    KRIS
Pretty much.
                    (Nods)
Based on what the automaton showed me, it was clear that there was a lot of disk thrashing between the CPU and the disk attached.

                    DAN
Which would have been alleviated with additional I/O channels.

                    KRIS
That's how I interpreted what I saw.

                    DAN
How about the automatons falling off the bridge, what do you think that was.

                    KRIS
Well, again, I kinda had the sense that I was in the midst of what was going on, but still an observer, so I made my way to the bridge, and was able to zoom a little further so that I could ask an automaton before it fell off the bridge, why it was doing what it was doing.

                    DAN
What did you find out?

                    KRIS
                    (Makes a gesture as if holding up a scroll)
Again, the automaton showed me what appeared to be collisions.

                    DAN
                    (Questioning)
Data packets?

KRIS
Yup, data packet collisions which caused a packet of data to be lost.
(Gestures with his hand)
Or, from my point of view, an automaton falling off a bridge.

DAN
Think about the potential.

KRIS
Don't I know it!
(Shakes his head affirmatively)
What I would have given on many occasions in my career to be able to diagnose computer problems by seeing them.

DAN
(Shakes his head in disbelief)
This experiment worked out so much better than I had hoped.

KRIS
Knowing you, you probably want to tinker a little more, but I think that the lovely contraption that you built,
(Blows a kiss in the direction of the chair in the middle of the stage)
is ready for prime time.

DAN
Do you really think so?

KRIS
(Emphatically)
Oh, absolutely!

DAN
So, how do we market this?

KRIS

I don't know, I guess we have to build some credibility first, 'ya know?

DAN
(Nods)
Yeah, it probably doesn't make a lot of sense
(Pointing to the chair)
wheeling that chair from company to company and trying to sell our idea that way.

KRIS
No, but we do have a solution for diagnosing computer problems.
(Pauses)
Lord knows, companies have computer problems.

DAN
(Pointing to the computer)
All we need to do is to find a company that has a problem with their computer.

KRIS
(Lifts his finger in the air)
Or computers.

DAN
(Nods in agreement)
Or computers.
(Pointing to Kris)
Because you said that you could leave the confines of one computer, so God only knows how many computers we can span.

KRIS
A data center?

DAN
A complete network?

                    KRIS
                (Questioning)
The complete Internet?

                    DAN
Why not!
                (Pondering)
I'd wager to say that every network has a computer or two that has at least one undiagnosed problem.

                    KRIS
            (Smiling from ear to ear)
Yeah, finding a company with computer problems will be like shooting fish in a barrel!

                    DAN
You're right.
                    (Nods)
Like you said before, first we gain credibility with a couple of clients, then we build from there.
                (Lifts his finger)
That's when we start making serious money!

                    KRIS
Dan,
            (With anticipation)
this is going to be good!
            (Dan is tapping his lips, clearly deep in thought)
So, what do you think our next step should be?

                    DAN
                (Smiles broadly)
Go to the bar!
                (Stands up)
I think that we have some celebrating to do!

(The lights dim as Dan and Kris are seen getting up from their chairs at the table, and giving each other an embrace.

Blackout and end of Act 1.)

Act I Scene 2

>(Six months later at a government installation. Dan and Kris are seated at one side of a table in a conference room. Dr. Hamilton, David and Larry are seated at the other side of the table, with Dr. Hamilton in the middle.
>
>Dr. Hamilton, David and Larry are looking at paper copies of a presentation that Dan and Kris have brought with them.
>
>In this scene:
>Dan, Kris, Dr. Hamilton, David, Larry)

                DR. HAMILTON
>(Flipping through the presentation and nodding his head)

Very impressive. Very impressive.
>(Looks over to David and Larry and asks them)

Larry. David. What do you think?

                LARRY
>(Looking at Dr. Hamilton)

Oh, I agree, Dr. Hamilton, this is very impressive; although,
>(Looking at Dan and Kris)

I have several questions I'd like to ask these gentlemen.

                DR. HAMILTON
>(Looking over at David)

What about you, David?

DAVID
(Looking at Dr. Hamilton)
Oh, I agree with Larry, Dr. Hamilton,
(Looking at Dan and Kris)
and I also have several questions that I would like to ask
(Motions with his hand to Dan and Kris)
these gentlemen.

DR. HAMILTON
(Addressing Dan and Kris)
As you can gather from everything you've seen at this facility from the time you arrived to the time that you were escorted into this conference room, this is a very secure location.
(Leans forward)
I would like to discuss your, your
(Pauses)
solution openly and honestly; although please don't be offended if we can't reciprocate and give you specific details in our responses. As you can imagine, we must be very cognizant of maintaining national security.
(Looking first at Dan, and then at Kris)
Do you understand?

DAN	KRIS
Yes, sir!	

DR. HAMILTON
(Nods)
Good!
(Looks to David and Larry)
Why don't we start asking questions?
(Looks at David)
David, why don't you go first?

DAVID
Sure, Dr. Hamilton.

> (Peering over his glasses at Dan and Kris)

Before I ask questions about your presentation, there is a fundamental question that I have to ask.

DAN
> (Sitting erect in his chair with his hands clasped together)

Okay.

DAVID

If you are permitted to take a little
> (Motions with his hands, puts emphasis on the word "excursion")

excursion into the computers here at this facility, will you be using anything that will
> (Puts emphasis on the words "record" and "transmit:)

record or *transmit* the data from this location to another location?

DAN

No sir.
> (Pauses)

The only transmission of information that will occur is the communication between my colleague, Kris
> (Points to Kris)

with his handheld device and me with the command console.

DAVID
> (Peers over the top of his glasses at Dan)

Please describe the kind of communication that will occur between the handheld device and the command console.

DAN

The primary reason for communicating with one another is so that Kris will have a place to record the issues that he finds while he is in the computer.

DAVID
Although, you mentioned that communication is bi-directional.

DAN
Yes, sir. We can communicate with one another using a simple text editor.

DAVID
(Gently tapping on the table with his finger)
Please give me a little more detail.

DAN
Well, again, the primary purpose of having the communication set up is not to communicate with one another per se; although, the primary reason of having the communication set up is so that I can watch on the console and see the issues that Kris has discovered with the computer.

DAVID
Kind of a log?

DAN
Exactly!

DR. HAMILTON
That's the log you reference once Kris comes out of the computer, correct?

DAN
(Addressing Dr. Hamilton)
That is correct, sir.

DAVID
So, is it fair to say that you will not be leaving this facility with any data?

                    DAN
            (Nods, addressing David)
Yes sir, it is fair to say that.

                    DAVID
You do have the capability of looking at all the components on the computer, correct?

                    DAN
Yes, sir we do.

                    DAVID
And I also presume that you can distinguish which of the components you are looking at.

                    DAN
            (Nodding affirmatively)
That is correct.

                    DAVID
            (Peering over his glasses and giving a sly smile)
So, how is it that if you go into the computer looking at the
            (Motions with his hand)
database, let's say, that you won't be able to record or transmit the data stored there.

                    KRIS
If we went into a database, I wouldn't be able to distinguish specific data values.

                    DAVID
Couldn't distinguish a data value?

                    KRIS
No sir.

DAVID
(In an irritated tone)
Well what good is that?

KRIS
(Questioning)
Sir?

DAVID
What if the problem
(Puts emphasis on the word "is")
is with the data? How valuable will your journey into the computer be if you can't distinguish a data value?

KRIS
(Nods)
Oh, I see your point.
(Looking directly at David)
Let me tell you step by step what would happen in a situation where there is a data related issue?

DAVID
(Sits back in his chair)
Please do.

KRIS
First off, if there is a data related issue,
(Pauses, still looking at David)
coming into the computer, I wouldn't know that.
(David nods)
What I would see would be a flurry of activity off in some location.

DAVID
(Still nodding)
Okay.

KRIS

Seeing that kind of activity would give me a reason to want to investigate the situation further.

(David is listening intently)

I would then zoom closer to the location where the activity is occurring.

DAVID
(Questioning)

Zoom?

KRIS

When I am in the computer I have the ability to zoom in or out on a specific area.

LARRY

Like a microscope?

KRIS
(Making eye contact with Larry)

Yes sir, exactly.

(Pauses)

I can zoom all the way out and see things from a broad perspective, and then as I see areas that attract my attention, I can zoom in until the point where I am in the midst of where the problem is actually occurring.

DAVID

So, when you are in the midst of the problem,

(Gestures with his hand)

or what appears to be the problem you then do what?

KRIS

I am able to see the problem directly.

(Pauses)

For example, if the problem is with the program code, then I can precisely see the line, or lines of code that are causing the problem.

Or, if there is a problem with a hardware component, I can be presented with a diagram of why the component is failing.
                         (Lifting a finger for emphasis)
If the issue happens to be with the data, then I would pinpoint that issue, and request to be presented with the offending data string, in which case I can see data corruption or data mismatch issues.

                         DAVID
Can you manipulate the lines of code or data?

                         KRIS
No sir, I can only observe, I can't modify anything.

                         DAVID
Is that out of design? Or do you choose not to modify anything?

                         KRIS
Sir, it is out of design, I cannot modify anything when I am in the computer.

                         DAVID
                       (Leans forward, looks over his glasses)
But, at no time when you're in the computer will you be retrieving, storing, or carrying data away with you.

                         KRIS
                         (Emphatically)
No sir, absolutely not, sir!

                         LARRY
                         (Questioning)
In and out of the computer?
                         (Pauses)
That sounds so odd to me, how is
                         (Pointing to Kris)
this young man going to go

(Puts emphasis on the words "in" and "out")

in or *out* of the computer?

KRIS

I don't go into the computer physically, sir, I only go into the computer virtually.

LARRY

So, what exactly does that mean?

(Smiles, looking at Kris)

It's been a lot of years since I've done anything technical, and Lord knows I don't play any of those computer games, so could you explain it so even a

(Puts emphasis on the word "manager")

manager could understand it?

KRIS

I will try, sir.

LARRY

(Leans forward and looks at Dan and Kris)

You both can call me Larry if you want.

DR. HAMILTON

(Looking at Dan and Kris)

That's right, guys.

(Pointing to the presentation)

The three of us have been reading about your successes over the last several months. It's obvious that you both have done something quite remarkable here.

(Gestures with his hand)

Something that no one else has ever done before. So,

(Pauses. Puts emphasis on the word "both")

believe me, you *both* have earned our respect, so you don't have to address us so formally.

                              KRIS
Thank you, Dr. Hamilton.
                    (Looking at Larry)
Larry, let me do my best to explain the sensation of going into the computer.
                 (Larry nods in anticipation)
The journey I take is a virtual journey which means that my body does not physically go into the computer. Physically my body does not leave the chair that hooks me up to the computer. The images and sounds that I see and hear are projected onto the virtual reality helmet which makes it appear to me that I am inside the computer. Virtual reality, in the sense that Dan and I are describing, is a set of techniques for creating an artificial, computer-generated environment in which I can enter into the computer.

                             LARRY
                          (Tentatively)
Okay.
                              DAN
              (Looking at the group across the table)
As you've mentioned, we've been doing this for several months now. Without exception,
                            (Pauses)
regardless of the operating system, computer size, computer hardware, or configuration of the network we have been able to virtually go into the computers and diagnose issues. Also, without exception, the computers that we have been hooked to have had problems,
                            (Pauses)
Can I assume that is the case with the computer system that you have here too?

                         DR. HAMILTON
That is correct, Dan.
                   (Looking at Larry and David)

                              151

I don't know if you guys would agree or not, but the complexity of our systems seems to be working against us. Our hardware and software vendors are all engaged in a finger pointing exercise.

LARRY
(Nodding affirmatively)

Oh, I would agree, with that all right, there are times when I think I'm on the set of the "Wizard of Oz",

> (Crosses his arms like the scarecrow on the "Wizard of Oz" and points in both directions)

with neither side accepting any blame.

DAVID
(Smiling)

Right.

(Pauses)

On top of the vendor representatives looking at our computer environment, we also have several very skilled people on staff who have also tried to diagnose the issues, all with little or no success.

DR. HAMILTON

Which is why, after reading about the continued success that you gentlemen have had with so many other clients, we thought that we would give you a call.

DAN

Well, I am confident that if you give us the opportunity to virtually enter into your computer environment that we can isolate the issues that are causing you the most grief.

LARRY

Not all the issues?

DAN

Well, a computer problem is not much different from problems that we experience in life.

LARRY
Dan, I'm not sure that I'm following you.

DAN
Well, let's say we have a problem with a person.

LARRY
Okay.

DAN
And let's say the person has a severe cut on their leg.

LARRY
Okay.

DAN
You or I would be able to identify the cut on the leg as being an issue which needed immediate attention.

LARRY
Sure.

DAN
While we were treating the cut on the leg, we probably wouldn't even notice that the person had an ingrown toenail.

LARRY
(Nods)
Even if we did notice it, we probably wouldn't give it a whole lot of thought when we were dealing with the immediate issue at hand.

DAN
Exactly!
(Pauses)
Although, once our patient is stabilized, and complained about a problem with their foot, we would then notice the ingrown toenail.

DAVID

Kinda like Kaizen.

DAN

Exactly!

LARRY

Ah, a process of continuous refinements!
(Pauses)
I see.

DR. HAMILTON

Are you saying then that you may need to go into the computer system multiple times?

DAN

Believe me, we can identify several problems on the initial inspection.

KRIS
(Nods in agreement, putting emphasis on the word "several")

Several problems!
(Pauses)
But to use the analogy that Dan was using prior, I don't want to give the impression that we will only be looking to identify the most critical issues. We will be looking to identify all issues.
(Shrugs)
Depending on how much time we have in the computer, we can identify all the visible problems.

DR. HAMILTON

Well, time is an issue.

DAN

How much time will we have?

DR. HAMILTON

One minute.

DAN
(Looking over at Kris)

What do you think, Kris?

KRIS
(Scribbling on a piece of paper)

Well, based on our experience, one minute
(Uses his hands to do air quotes when he says "on the outside")
"on the outside" will give me nearly one day of time inside the computer to do the research, which should be more than enough to identify the significant issues.

DR. HAMILTON
(Looking at Kris)

What's your sense of confidence that you can find a significant problem or series of problems in that time?

KRIS

My sense of confidence is very high.

DAN

So is mine.

DR. HAMILTON

The information we've been reading indicates that your success rate is one hundred percent.
(Pauses)
Do you think that you are going to keep your streak alive?

KRIS

Absolutely!

DR. HAMILTON

(Looking at Dan)
What about you, Dan?

DAN
(Looking at Dr. Hamilton)
If I didn't think we could do the job in the time allotted, I would tell you
(Looking at the group)
I believe that we can identify many significant problems in a minute.

LARRY
(Shaking his head and looking at his colleagues)
How many months have we invested in trying to find the bugs already?

DR. HAMILTON
(Looking at Larry)
A long time.
(Pauses)
Too long!

DAVID
Who owns the logs created during the session?

DAN
We will give you the logs so that you have something to go by in order to make the modifications.

DAVID
Tell me this.

DAN
Okay.

DAVID

When we look at your logs will we be able to identify a specific component as the problem?

DAN

Absolutely!
    (Pauses)
We will be able to tell you whether the problem is software related, whether it is a chip on the motherboard, whether it is a specific card, you name it.
    (Looking over at Kris)
We will identify the problem.

LARRY

What if the problem is with a component that you may not normally suspect, say like a
    (Pauses)
a power cord?

KRIS
    (Smiling and looking at Dan)
Oh, we've found problems like that before.

LARRY

So, how would you find a problem like that?
    (Pauses)
Wouldn't it be a needle in a haystack?

KRIS

Using conventional techniques, it would probably be impossible to find.
    (Pauses)
With the method that Dan and I are presenting, finding obscure problems become easy.

LARRY

How?

(Puts his finger to his lips)
I mean wouldn't you have to make your way through an entire data center,
(Extends his hand)
and then hunt around before you found the problem?

KRIS

Well, Larry, think about it like this.
(Pauses)
When I first enter the computer I am always zoomed all the way out.

LARRY
(Questions)
Zoomed like with a microscope like we talked about before?

KRIS

Exactly! Another way to think of it is that you might imagine a traffic helicopter looking around the freeway system for potential problem areas. The helicopter is zoomed out so the pilot can see a broad expanse.
(Larry nods with comprehension)
Like the helicopter pilot, I don't know, when I first come into the computer where the problems are, so I continue to walk around,
(Lifts his finger for emphasis)
fully zoomed out, until I see something that stands out as being out of place.

LARRY
(With understanding)
Ah, okay.

KRIS

Then, once I find something that appears to be out of place, I will zoom in until I get to a level where I can make some sense of what it is that I am seeing.

DAVID

So, let's take this example of the bad power cord,
>   (Shakes his head and says uncertainly)
how do you find that the problem is with the power cord?

                              KRIS
When I zoom all the way in, I can see some degree of disorder with the,
>   (Waves with his hand)
let's call them particles, that are traveling in the power cord.

                         DR. HAMILTON
With the particles?

                              KRIS
Yes.

                         DR. HAMILTON
So, you're at the atomic level?

                              DAN
Amazing, isn't it?

                         DR. HAMILTON
Yeah, but if….
>   (Pauses)
If you consider the Heisenberg Uncertainty Principal, isn't there an impact being at the atomic level and observing something also at the atomic level?

                              DAN
Funny you should ask that because that question also had me tied in knots too.

                         DR. HAMILTON
I would think so.
>   (Shrugs)

I mean as you know, according to the Uncertainty Principal you can modify a particle by observing it.

DAN

And do you know what I've concluded?

DR. HAMILTON
(Curiously)

No. What?

DAN

I've concluded that if we were physically at the atomic level viewing something, then in fact we would modify the objects' behavior, as the Uncertainty Principal states.

DR. HAMILTON

Of course!

DAN

However, since we are virtually at the atomic level, and
(Lifts his finger in the air and puts emphasis on the word "not")
not physically at the atomic level, then we do not influence what we are observing.

DR. HAMILTON
(Chuckles)

I'm glad you offered that conclusion, Dan, because that would have also twisted me in knots until I came to the same conclusion.
(Nodding affirmatively)
What you said makes sense.

DAN
(Smiles)

Great minds think alike.

DR. HAMILTON

(Gesturing to Dan)
Clearly, you have a great mind to have come up with something so amazing.

DAN
(Bows his head graciously and sincerely says)
Thank you!

DAVID
Can I assume that since you are
(Puts emphasis on the word "zoomed")
zoomed in at the atomic level that you can pass freely between the different devices when you need to.

KRIS
Oh yeah, there are no obstacles at all.

DAVID
Because I've had this gnawing question about how you will cross through our virtual hardware partitions
(Lifts his finger for emphasis)
or more importantly, our firewalls into secure portions of the network.

KRIS
(Pointing to Dan)
As Dan mentioned, some of the restrictions are not in force simply because this is a virtual journey into the computer.

DAVID
(Looking at his wristwatch)
You guys did a great job explaining everything, and I do have to agree with what Dr. Hamilton said earlier,
(Looking at Dan and Kris)
you both certainly have done something quite remarkable, and you have my respect.

LARRY
(Looking at Dan and Kris)
Mine too!

DR. HAMILTON
(Looking at David and Larry)
Do you guys have any other questions?

(The lights fade with the individuals in the scene still gathered around the table.

Blackout and end of Act 1.)

Act II Scene 1

(Similar to the opening of the play, Dan is standing beside Kris who is sitting in an elaborate contraption that looks somewhat like a dentist chair. Kris is holding a handheld electronic device which is hooked up to a computer via a tangle of wires that encircles him.

The backdrop behind Dan and Kris indicates that they are in a massive data center.

In this scene:
Dan, Kris and Dr. Hamilton)

DAN
(Checking the connections between Kris and the handheld device)

This is it.

KRIS
(Sounding a little preoccupied)

Huh?

DAN
(Excitedly)

This is it!
(Smiles)
This is the break we've been waiting for!

KRIS

No doubt about it.
(Looking around with limited mobility)
We're definitely in the big league now.

                    DAN
              (Shaking his head in disbelief)
Hard to believe!

              (Checking the connections between Kris
              and handheld device again)
How do your connections feel?

                    KRIS
A-okay, captain.
              (Pauses)
Hey.

                    DAN
Yeah?

                    KRIS
              (Moving his head to look at Dan)
You've gotta try this one day.

                    DAN
              (Looks over at the command console,
              and then back to Kris)
'Ya know what?

                    KRIS
What?

                    DAN
I was thinking about trying it today.

                    KRIS
              (Surprised)
You were?

                    DAN
              (Nodding)
Yeah,

(Pauses)

Honestly.

                              KRIS
                        (Sincerely)

'Ya wanna swap?

                              DAN
                      (Looking at Kris)

Not this time, although,

                        (Pauses)

how about next time?

                              KRIS

Sure.

                        (Hesitantly)

Although,

                              DAN

Yeah?

                              KRIS

If this really is the big time, and if we both get rich doing this then….

                              DAN

Yeah?

                              KRIS

We may not be doing this much longer together.

                              DAN
                        (Softly)

I know.

                              KRIS

We'll be contacting other people to go into computers and diagnose computer problems.

DAN
(Shaking his finger)
Well, I'll give this contraption a ride once or twice before I allow that to happen.

KRIS
(Excitedly)
Oh Dan, you have to!
(Pauses)
I mean,
(Pauses)
I do such a bad job describing what it's really like in there.
(Strains to look at Dan)
You really do have to try this.

DAN
Well, if we weren't on such a tight window today, I'd ask to take your place.

KRIS
How much time do we have?

DAN
(Looking at his watch)
Just about five minutes.
(Pauses)
And you know.

CHIRS
Huh?

DAN
You know we're on a tight deadline today, right?

KRIS

Oh, I remember.

(Pauses)

I've got a minute.

(Putting emphasis on the word "you")

Or, should I say *you* have a minute.

DAN

Yeah.

(Shaking his head)

That still amazes me.

KRIS

What, the time difference?

DAN

Exactly!

(Pauses)

I mean, I did anticipate a time difference based on the way the equipment is synched to the computer time; although, it still surprises me.

KRIS

You'd be amazed at how much you can do in a short amount of clock time.

DAN

(With emphasis)

I've been amazed.

(Pauses)

Each time you come out after being in the computer for ten, fifteen, or twenty seconds I am amazed when I look at the logs and see how much you accomplish in that time.

(Pauses)

'Ya know what?

KRIS

What?

DAN

The first time I was almost convinced that you were playing a trick on me.

KRIS

You were?

DAN

Honest. I was.

KRIS

When did you realize that I wasn't playing a trick on you?

DAN

When I read the logs. It would have been impossible,
(Puts emphasis on the word "impossible")
I mean *impossible* for you to have written the logs with such detail.

KRIS
(Surprised)

So, you thought that I was pulling your leg?

DAN
(Nodding)

Yup! I really did.

KRIS
(Starts to chuckle)

Dan, that's hilarious!

DAN

It's true. That first time, I was
(Pauses)

skeptical. I mean,
(Pauses)
I mean don't get me wrong.

KRIS

Yeah.

DAN

I was expecting that the experiment would be a success, but never,
(Shaking his head)
never did I think the experiment would be so successful to get us to the opportunity that we have here today.

KRIS

No question,
(Pauses)
I agree.

DAN

We're lucky, Kris.

KRIS
(In agreement)
Very lucky!

DAN
(Sounding concerned)
Do you think you'll have enough time?

KRIS

To find the problem?

DAN

Yeah.

KRIS

No doubt about it. I'll have more than enough time.

(Pauses)
I promise to monitor the time very carefully,
(Pauses)
don't worry. We've got this!

DAN
I guess I'm a little concerned because we've never been under a time constraint like this.

KRIS
(Reassuringly)
Dan don't worry. The time shouldn't be an issue.
(Pauses)
From my perspective, I'll have plenty of time, but I'll still

KRIS	DAN
Keep an eye on the time.	

KRIS
(Chuckles)
That's right, boss, I'll have an eye on the time.

DAN
And keep your other eye on the console.

KRIS
Dan?

DAN
Yeah?

KRIS
(With a smile)
I've only got two eyes.

DAN

                 (Nodding)
Yeah, I know.
                 (Playfully)
So, what's your point?

                    KRIS
Well, if one eye is on the time, and one eye is on the consoles,
                 (Pauses)
how am I supposed to identify any problems with the computers?

                    DAN
                 (Smiles)
You know what I mean, Bozo!

                    KRIS
Why are you so concerned?

                    DAN
Well, I guess because this is the big opportunity that we were waiting for, and
                 (Pauses)
to be honest, I don't know what would happen if you were in the computer when it was rebooting?

                    KRIS
Relax, Grandma.

                    DAN
                 (Chuckles. Puts emphasis on the word "grandma")

Grandma, is it?

                 (A beep is heard indicating that someone else is coming through the security doors into the computer room. The sound of a door opening and shutting is heard. The sound of approaching footsteps is also heard. Dan leans toward Kris and whispers.)

Someone's coming.

                    KRIS

Who do you think it is?

                    (Pauses)

Darth Vader?

                    DAN
         (Catching a glimpse of Dr. Hamilton)

Dr. Hamilton, we're honored that you would come.

                    KRIS
              (Softly muttering)

I was wrong.

              (Speaking normally)

Dr. Hamilton, thank you for coming.

                DR. HAMILTON

To be honest I have two reasons for coming.

                    DAN
                (Questioning)

Sir?

                DR. HAMILTON

The first reason is pragmatic.

                (Pauses)

I needed to tell you precisely when you can enter the computer.

                    DAN

Okay.

                DR. HAMILTON

And to be honest.

DAN

Yes?

DR. HAMILTON

My second reason for coming is out of curiosity.
(Shaking his head in awe looking at the device)
I'd like to see for myself how this works.

DAN

Well, to get a real feel for how it works, you'd have to switch places with
(Pointing to Kris)
Kris, since he'll be the one having all the fun.

DR. HAMILTON
(In agreement)
It does sound like fun.
(Pauses)
One day I'd like to try it myself.

DAN

Me too.

DR. HAMILTON

Oh, you've never tried it?

DAN

No,
(Pointing to Kris)
I've let Kris have all the fun.

KRIS
(Leaning over and looking at Dr. Hamilton and Dan)
No disagreement here,

>   (Excitedly, putting emphasis on the word
>   "is")

This *is* fun!

>   DR. HAMILTON
>   (Smiling)

One day you'll have to give us a turn.

>   KRIS
>   (Hesitantly)

Well, maybe.

>   DAN
>   (Looking at Dr. Hamilton, pointing to
>   Kris)

Do you see what I have to put up with?

>   DR. HAMILTON
>   (Chuckles)

You guys are fun to work with, no doubt about that!

>   DAN

Thanks, Dr. Hamilton.

>   DR. HAMILTON

Are you guys ready?

>   DAN

All I have to do is put on the virtual reality helmet, and Kris will be ready to go.

>   DR. HAMILTON

We should get Kris ready, since I will be getting a phone call which will tell me when Kris will be cleared to enter into the computer.

>   DAN

> (Walking over to the VR helmet, looks at Kris)

Are you ready for me to put the helmet on?

KRIS

What? No kiss goodbye?

DAN
> (Dr. Hamilton chuckles, as Dan starts to put the VR helmet on Kris. Dan smiles and addresses Dr. Hamilton)

This guy is incorrigible!

DR. HAMILTON

You guys make a great team!

DAN
> (Focusing on putting the VR helmet on Kris, in agreement)

Yeah, I kinda think so too.
> (Pointing to Kris)

He's not the best looking guy to work with, but he's a good guy.

KRIS
> (Putting emphasis on the word "hear")

I can still *hear* you!

DR. HAMILTON

Do you guys always have this much fun?

DAN

We try to.

DR. HAMILTON
> (A cell phone is heard ringing)

Excuse me.

(Reaches into his pocket, takes out the phone and answers it.)

Hello, this is Dr. Hamilton.

(Nods speaking to the person on the phone)

Okay, so I will go through a count down with you, right?

(Looking over at Dan)

Are you guys ready?

DAN
(Nodding)

Yes.

DR. HAMILTON

We'll be ready in a couple of seconds, and then I'll count down from five.

DAN

Okay.

KRIS

I'll press engage when I hear you say "zero".

DR. HAMILTON

(Speaking to the person on the phone)

Yes. Yes, that's right they are ready and waiting for the countdown.

(Pauses. Still talking to the person on the phone)

Okay, okay.

(Cups the phone and talks to Dan and Kris)

We're getting close, guys, I'll start the countdown from five in a second.

(Speaking to the person on the phone)

Yes, that's right, we'll countdown together from five.

(Pauses)

Okay, here we go. Five. Four. Three. Two. One. Zero.

KRIS

Engage.

(The lights dim, as Dan and Dr. Hamilton turn their attention to the command console. Blackout and end of Act II, Scene 1)

Act II Scene 2

>(Against a backdrop of what appears to be frosted opaque glass there are a series of lights which randomly blink on an off.[1]
>
>Kris is swiftly walking across the stage.
>
>In this scene:
>Kris and Zia)

           ZIA

Hey!

           KRIS
>(Stops dead in his tracks)

Huh?

>(Looking around)

Who said that?

           ZIA
>(Motioning with her hand)

Over here.

           KRIS
>(Startled. Turning and looking at Zia)

Who are you?

           ZIA

My name is Zia.
>(Pauses)

What's your name?

           KRIS
>(Stunned)

---

[1] A black background with a series of multi-color lights mounted on to the background covered by a frosted opaque glass.

Kris. My name is Kris.
                              (Pauses, tentatively walks towards Zia)
I guess I meant to say how….
                              (Pauses)
how did you get inside the computer?

                              ZIA
Same way you did, I guess.

                              KRIS
                            (Shaking his head negatively)
No,
                              (Pauses)
no, I don't think so.

                              ZIA
Sure, I did.

                              KRIS
Are you a part of the computer?

                              ZIA
                            (Starts to walk closer to Kris)
Part of the computer?
                              (Pauses)
No. Not any more than you are.

                              KRIS
I'm in the computer, but not
                              (Pauses)
not a part of it.

                              ZIA
                            (Still walking closer to Kris)
So, you've never seen anyone on your voyages before?

                              KRIS

Oh sure,
>(Pauses)

sure I have, but it's just
>(Pauses)

just that no one in the computer has ever spoken to me before.
>(Pauses)

I don't know if you've seen them before, the….
>(Pauses)

well, I call them automatons that I see in the computer.

ZIA

Oh, I know what you're talking about!

KRIS

>(Puzzled)

You do?
>(As if enlightened)

Oh, I get it you're like the person in charge of those automatons.

ZIA

I am?

KRIS

>(Shrugs)

I wasn't making a statement, I was just
>(Pauses)

just guessing.

ZIA

Well did you ever touch one of the automatons?
>(Pauses)

Do you know what they feel like?

KRIS

No, the
>(Pauses)

the automatons wouldn't let me touch them.

                  ZIA
              (Softly)

Give me your hand, Kris.

                 KRIS

What?

                  ZIA
              (Calmly)

Give me your hand, Kris.

                 KRIS

I'll be zapped if I do that.

                  ZIA
            (Questioning)

You'll be what?

                 KRIS

Zapped!

             (Pauses)

You know,

             (Shrugs)

electrocuted.

                  ZIA
            (Smiling)

Don't be silly.

            (Extending her hand to Kris)

Give me your hand,

             (Pauses)

please.

                 KRIS
            (Timidly)

But won't that kill me?

                    ZIA
            (Shakes her head negatively)
No.
                    (Pauses)
Trust me, Kris.

                    KRIS
            (Tentatively reaches out his hand)
I don't know, I kinda have a bad feeling about this.

                    ZIA
            (Moving her hand closer to Kris' hand)
Why?

                    KRIS
I guess because,
                    (Pauses)
I guess because I'm afraid.

                    ZIA
            (Looking at Kris in the eyes)
Trust me.

                    KRIS
            (Walks around Zia and checks her out)
You look normal enough.

                    ZIA
Thanks,
                    (Smiles)
so do you.

                    KRIS
                    (Puzzled)
So, why do I have to touch your hand?

ZIA

Because you said that you never spoke with anyone on your voyages before. I just wanted to

(Pauses)

just wanted to show you that I'm not any different than you.

KRIS
(Reaches out his hand)

Why do I feel as though I'm going to regret this?

ZIA
(Reassuringly)

Trust me, Kris.

KRIS
(Moves his hand forward and taps Zia's hand briefly)

Hey.

ZIA

See! You didn't get zapped!

(Smiles)

I didn't trick you.

KRIS
(Reaches out and firmly puts his hand on Zia's hand)

You're solid.

ZIA
(Looking at Kris)

Just like you.

KRIS
(Moves his hand back, and walks around Zia again)

How can you feel solid if I'm only here virtually?

ZIA
Because we are occupying the same space and time.

KRIS
(Puzzled)
We're doing what?

ZIA
We're occupying the same space and time, Kris.
(Pauses)
You see it every once in a while when you take a virtual journey.

KRIS
(Shaking his head)
Honestly, it's never happened to me before.
(Pauses)
So, what does it mean?

ZIA
Well, as I'm sure you know, when the boundary of one plane intersects with another, it causes a wrinkle in the space time fabric.

KRIS
Kinda like parallel universes?

ZIA
Kinda, but
(Pauses)
by definition there is only one Universe.

KRIS
So, how did we end up here together?

ZIA
It happens. It happens a lot in the real world too.

KRIS

It does?

ZIA

Absolutely,
        (Pauses)
more often than you might imagine in the real world, it's just
        (Pauses)
with everything in the real world, it's not always easy to see when you're at a space time boundary.

KRIS

What would coming to a
        (Tentatively says the word "boundary")
boundary in the real world look like?

ZIA

Well,
        (Pauses)
I don't claim to be an expert, but as I'm sure you know time proceeds differently on these virtual voyages than it does in the real world, right?

KRIS
(Nodding)

Sure.

ZIA

So, in the real world when two boundaries intersect you will see a small, momentary, almost imperceptible flash of light.

KRIS
(Questioning)

Really?

ZIA

Yeah.

(Nodding)
Kinda just like a bright pinpoint of light.

KRIS

Just a pinpoint of light?

ZIA

Yeah, but against the background of the real world, it's sometimes difficult to see.

KRIS

You know, I think I've seen a couple of quick bursts of light before,
(Pauses)
but I never really gave it much thought.

ZIA

Well, it's very possible that you've come to a space time boundary before.

KRIS

Even so,
(Pauses)
Zia you might think that I'm really stupid, but I don't have a clue what you're talking about.

ZIA

Well, it really doesn't matter.
(Pauses)
The important thing to know is that since you and I have come to this boundary together we can choose to go either way.

KRIS

Either way?

ZIA

I can come into your dimension or you can come into mine.

KRIS
If you came into my dimension, how would I find you?

ZIA
I would come with you.

KRIS
But I'm only here virtually.

ZIA
Me too, but if I went with you, I would then occupy your dimension and
(Pauses)
appear in your dimension.

KRIS
Virtually?

ZIA
No, I would physically be in your dimension.
(Reassuringly)
Like I said, it happens more often than you might think.

KRIS
I guess I'm having a rough time understanding how
(Putting emphasis on the word "it")
it happens.

ZIA
Coming to the intersection of one dimension with another.

KRIS
Okay,
(Pauses)
hold it right there. Do you mean to say that you and I are from different dimensions?

ZIA

Well, yeah.

(Nodding)

Absolutely.

KRIS

You're not from planet Earth?

ZIA

In my dimension, the place I come from may be the same physical space as where you are from, but we do

(Shaking her head negatively)

not call our place,

(Carefully saying the word "earth")

earth.

KRIS

(Shaking his head)

Freaky.

ZIA

What?

KRIS

The whole notion is so strange to me.

ZIA

Believe me, I can understand that.

KRIS

I mean

(Pauses)

I mean, I'm a computer guy, not some, some

(Emphasizes the phrase "space traveler")

space traveler.

ZIA
You and I didn't travel through space, Kris,
(Softly)
we're just from different dimensions.

KRIS
So, you said that you can come into my dimension and I can come into your dimension?

ZIA
Yes.

KRIS
Wouldn't I cease to exist if I crossed into your
(Carefully says "dimension")
dimension?

ZIA
No, not really,
(Pauses)
although....

KRIS
Yeah?

ZIA
You can only be in one dimension
(Shrugs)
but that's kind of obvious, huh?

KRIS
But what about my body
(Tentatively says the word "if")
if I were to come with you? What would happen to my physical body?

                             ZIA
Your physical body can't simultaneously occupy two dimensions, so
your physical body in your dimension would die.

                             KRIS
How does my body get transferred from one dimension to another?

                             ZIA
I'm not going to pretend that I know the details, it's something about
the holographic nature of the Universe.

                             KRIS
                       (Shaking his head)
Transferring from one dimension to another,
                           (Shrugs)
just like that.

                             ZIA
                        (Reassuringly)
Kris, each of us are the result of a series of possibilities.
                     (Motions with her hand)
I am the result of one set of possibilities, and you are the result of
another set of possibilities.

                             KRIS
Set of possibilities?

                             ZIA
Yeah,
                           (Pauses)
it's kind of mind boggling when you think of it.

                             KRIS
Mind Boggling? Heck,
                       (Shaking his head)
I don't even understand what it means.

ZIA

Well, it's really very simple.

KRIS

The simpler the better.
(Pauses)
Can you try and explain it to me?

ZIA

Sure.
(Takes a breath)
But before I do that why don't you tell me a little about yourself.

KRIS

About myself?

ZIA

Yeah. For example, are you married? Do you have any kids?
(Shrugs)
That sort of thing.

KRIS

Well, I'm not married.

ZIA
(Quickly)
Good! What else.

KRIS

Not a whole lot, I mean I've been working a lot with my friend Dan on this experiment.

ZIA
(Questioning)
And that's how you got here?

               KRIS
Yeah.
               (Pauses)
Dan invented this,
               (Pauses)
this device that brought me here.

               ZIA
He sounds like a smart guy.

               KRIS
               (Nodding affirmatively)
Oh, he is!
               (Pauses)
Probably the smartest guy I've ever met.
               (Motions with his hand)
He's also got a great sense of humor.

               ZIA
It sounds like you really like your friend.

               KRIS
I do.

               ZIA
               (Takes a breath)
Okay, well imagine if you never met Dan, how would your life have been different?

               KRIS
I wouldn't be here now,
               (Pauses)
and I wouldn't have a great friend.

               ZIA

So, meeting Dan was one situation which brought about a series of possibilities for you in your life.

KRIS
Okay, I can see that.
(Pauses)
My life would have been entirely different if I didn't meet Dan.

ZIA
Your life would also have been different if you met someone and got married, right?

KRIS
No question.
(Pauses)
There was a time when I thought I would get married.

ZIA
Really?

KRIS
Yeah, I met a person when I was younger, and thought that she might be
(Puts emphasis on the phrase "the one")
the one, since we really connected as friends.
(Pauses)
Do you know what I mean?

ZIA
(Nodding)
Sure.
(Curiously)
It didn't work out?

KRIS
Well, I was young,
(Pauses)

I mean just a teenager, and
(Softly)
and her family moved away.

ZIA

I see.
(Pauses)
So, can you imagine how that one event brought about a different set of possibilities for you in your life?

KRIS

Sure.

ZIA

Each person we meet, each event that we are involved in, each decision that we make has an infinite number of outcomes.
(Pauses)
Those different outcomes are what makes your dimension and my dimension so vastly different.

KRIS
(Putting emphasis on the word "infinite")
An *infinite* set of outcomes?

ZIA

Oh absolutely.

KRIS

Why so many?

ZIA

Well, think about the possible number of outcomes that every event has.

KRIS

I guess it depends on the event and the number of people involved.

                          ZIA
Well,
                        (Pauses)
think about it.

                          KRIS
I understand that a person can make many choices.

                          ZIA
                        (Nodding)
And, in turn those choices bring with them a different set of outcomes.
                  (Lifting her hand for emphasis)
Compound that with the degree of randomness in everything we do, and then compound that again by all the people who are also making choices, then effected by randomness and uncertainty, believe me,
                  (Looking at Kris and emphasizing the
                  word "lot")
you've got a *lot* of choices.

                          KRIS
I guess I can see that.
                        (Pauses)
Are you some sort of scientist?

                          ZIA
                        (Smiling)
No.
                    (Looking at Kris)
Do I sound like one?

                          KRIS
You're teaching me a lot, Zia.

                          ZIA
Thanks.
                        (Pauses)

Just some things I've picked up along the way.

KRIS

So,
(Pauses. Looking at Zia)
for the sake of argument.

ZIA

Yes.

KRIS
(Puts emphasis on the word "if")

If I were to go with you.

ZIA

Yes.

KRIS

What would I expect?

ZIA

Well, it would be like starting fresh.

KRIS

Fresh?

ZIA

Yeah.
(Pauses)
What makes your dimension different from my dimension is all the different histories resulting from the different outcomes.

KRIS

Give me an example.

ZIA

The history of your dimension is different from the history of my dimension because of the different choices that people made along the way.

                    KRIS
Would there be the same people?

                    ZIA
              (Shaking her head negatively)
No.

                    KRIS
Why not?

                    ZIA
Some of the choices involve other people.
              (Pauses)
If your grandfather never married your grandmother, you wouldn't be here, right?

                    KRIS
Sure.

                    ZIA
So, there would be a totally different history of events,
              (Opens her right hand)
one with you, and
              (Opens her left hand)
one without you,
              (Closes her hands. Looking at Kris)
right?

                    KRIS
I guess so.
              (Softly)
Where does God fit into all this set of possibilities and randomness?

ZIA
(Shrugs)

Well.

KRIS

God exists in your dimension, doesn't He?

ZIA
(Emphatically)

Of course!
(Pauses)

As with the Universe, there is only one, by definition, the same is true with God.
(Pauses)

There is only One. But not being a theologian, I wouldn't have any better answer than you.

KRIS

Do you believe in God?

ZIA

Of course!
(Softly)

Do you?

KRIS

Of course!
(Moves closer to Zia)

Zia?

ZIA

Yes.

KRIS

Are you married?

ZIA

No.

        (Pauses)

I guess I never met

        (Puts emphasis on the phrase "the one")

the one for me

        (Pauses)

yet.

        (Looking at Kris)

Or maybe I have.

        (Pauses for a while before softly saying)

You seem very special, Kris.

KRIS
(Looking into Zia's eyes)
You seem very special too, Zia.

ZIA
I don't think we met by accident, Kris, I think
        (Pauses)
I think we were meant to meet one another.

KRIS
Would I see you if I came with you to your dimension?

ZIA
See me?
        (Pauses)
You mean like spend time with me and date me?

KRIS
(Sheepishly, looking at the floor)
Yes, I guess you can say that.

ZIA
(Emphatically)
Kris, I'd like that.

                          KRIS

So would I, Zia.
                          (Moves closer to Zia)

So would I.
                          (The stage lights start to dim and the
                          lights in background start to blink as
                          with a slowly pulsing strobe light.)

What's that?

                          ZIA

That means that there will be a disconnect between your dimension and my dimension soon.

                          KRIS

How soon?

                          ZIA

Soon, Kris.
                          (Looking at Kris)

Soon.
                          (Pauses)

Will you come with me to my dimension?

                          KRIS

Leave my dimension behind?

                          ZIA

I'll be with you, Kris.
                          (Pauses)

Just like before, you have to trust me.
                          (Moving closer to Kris)

I didn't mislead you before, and I won't mislead you now.
                          (Pauses)

Will you come with me?

                          KRIS

I'll never see you again if I go back to my dimension, right?

ZIA

That's right, Kris.

(Pauses)

Will you come with me?

(Kris' hand held device starts to beep, and the strobe lights start to pulse a little faster. Pointing to the handheld device that Kris is holding)

What's that?

KRIS

A communication device.

(Looking at the screen)

Someone from my dimension is telling me that I have to get out of the computer soon, or it will reboot.

ZIA

How do you get out?

KRIS

(Pointing to the disengage button on the handheld device)

By pressing this disengage button.

(Pauses)

Zia?

ZIA

Yes.

KRIS

If I do go back to my dimension, will I remember you?

ZIA

Of course, Kris.

(Pauses)

We will remember each other knowing that there is no way that we will ever see one another again.
    (The strobe lights start to blink a little faster. Softly)
Will you come with me Kris?
    (Looking into Kris' eyes)
We met for a reason.

KRIS
    (Pauses. Looks at Zia and then motions to his handheld device)
I need to enter something into my handheld device.
    (Starts typing on his handheld device with a stylus)
How much time do you think we have left?

ZIA
Not much, Kris.
    (Pauses)
Soon the portal will close for both of us.

(The stage lights are off as the strobe lights, now blinking very rapidly, continue to illuminate Kris and Zia who are frozen in place. Blackout and end of Act II, Scene 2)

Act II Scene 3

(The set for this scene is exactly the same set used in the beginning of the play. Dan is standing in the middle of the stage as a beam of light is directed on Dan with the rest of the stage not fully illuminated. Gradually, the stage lights come up.

In this scene:
Dan)

DAN

What quantifies success?

(Shrugs)

With the use of the notes from Kris' logs, we were able to diagnose the problems that Dr. Hamilton had with the computers at his installation.

(Laughs)

I can see why Larry said that meeting with the vendors looked like the set from the Wizard of Oz

(Crosses his arms and points both ways)

with all the finger pointing.

(Shakes his head)

Wow!

(Pauses)

What a can of worms!

(Shakes his head in dismay)

Those guys would have never uncovered all the problems that we discovered without the

(Points to the chair)

journey that Kris took into the computers at their complex.

(Starts to walk around the stage looking into the audience. Softly)

What constitutes success?

(Shrugging)

Fixing the problems that we set out to fix?
> (Nods)

I suppose so.
> (Continuing to walk as he talks)

I suppose so.
> (Pauses)

Although, I guess....
> (His voice starts to quiver)

Although, I guess I never knew the price of success.
> (Stops walking. Looks into the audience and is silent for a moment. Speaking normally)

Kris was a heroic traveler, a knowledgeable colleague, and most important of all a friend.
> (Nodding solemnly, and softly says)

A good friend.
> (Stands motionless for a moment and looks at the chair. Speaking normally. Starts walking again)

A good friend with a great sense of humor.
> (Pauses)

Kris wrote some things in his last journal entry that helped us fix the problems and
> (Pauses)

then for some reason he set about writing a message to me.
> (Pauses)

It was probably about the same time when I was writing him, begging him, pleading with him to disengage.
> (Pauses)

I knew that the computer was going to reboot soon and wanted to get Kris out of the computer, since I didn't know what would happen to him if he was in the computer when it rebooted.
> (Pauses)

I know now.
> (Lowers his head)

I know now what happens.
> (Lifts his finger in the air)

I just came back from my friend Kris' funeral.
                            (Pointing to the chair)
He was in the chair still engaged to the computer when it rebooted, and when the computer rebooted Kris' vital signs all flat lined.
                            (Shaking his head)
Not gradually.
                            (Softly)
All at once, the vital signs just went to zero.
                            (Walks silently for a moment. Speaking normally)
Although,
                            (Optimistically)
although, I have reason to believe that Kris did not die.
                            (Pauses)
Odd as it may sound, I believe that Kris is still alive in an
                            (Motions with his hands)
alternate dimension.
                            (Softly)
An alternate dimension.
                            (Stands motionless for a moment tapping his lip. Speaking normally)
The way he described it made it sound so enticing.
                            (Walking towards the chair)
As strange as it sounds,
                            (Shaking his head)
I mean I can't get over it, but when Kris was on his last voyage he met someone from another dimension and chose to go with her to that dimension.
                            (Sits in the chair)
His description was fascinating.
                            (Shaking his head exclaims)
Absolutely fascinating!
                            (Pauses)
It made me think whether or not I should do some exploration myself.
                            (Leaning back in the chair with the VR helmet within reach)

Actually, I'm surprised I waited this long to take a voyage into the computer.

> (Reaches for the handheld device and sets it on his chest)

I'm not sure if I will come to a cross-dimensional boundary like Kris did; although, if nothing else, the journey into the computer sounds very cool!

> (Puts the VR helmet on and grasps the handheld device)

Wow! This is cool!

> (Sits motionless for a moment. Emphatically)

Engage!

(Blackout. End of play. Curtain.)

Made in the USA
Monee, IL
16 March 2024